THE NEGLECTED ASPECT

OF FOREIGN AFFAIRS

The Neglected Aspect of Foreign Affairs

American Educational and Cultural Policy Abroad

Charles Frankel

THE BROOKINGS INSTITUTION *Washington, D.C.*

THE BROOKINGS INSTITUTION is an independent organization devoted to nonpartisan research, education, and publication in economics, government, foreign policy, and the social sciences generally. Its principal purposes are to aid in the development of sound public policies and to promote public understanding of issues of national importance.

The Institution was founded December 8, 1927, to merge the activities of the Institute for Government Research, founded in 1916, the Institute of Economics, founded in 1922, and the Robert Brookings Graduate School of Economics and Government, founded in 1924.

The general administration of the Institution is the responsibility of a self-perpetuating Board of Trustees. The trustees are likewise charged with maintaining the independence of the staff and fostering the most favorable conditions for creative research and education. The immediate direction of the policies, program, and staff of the Institution is vested in the President, assisted by the division directors and an advisory council, chosen from the professional staff of the Institution.

In publishing a study, the Institution presents it as a competent treatment of a subject worthy of public consideration. The interpretations and conclusions in such publications are those of the author or authors, and do not purport to represent the views of the other staff members, officers, or trustees of the Brookings Institution.

BOARD OF TRUSTEES

Foreword

THE TRADITION OF cultural exchange across political boundaries is as old as the history of civilization, but the postwar growth of both public and private exchange programs has reached a scale and significance undreamed of a few decades ago. The flow of governmentally supported American scholars going abroad has increased from a mere trickle before the war to a current rate of about 2,000 a year. The traffic of foreign scholars coming to the United States has grown to about 5,000 a year. This crossing of national frontiers via numerous cultural bridges is increasingly important, not only as an end in itself but as a major force in governmental relations. International projects related to geophysical collaboration, arms control, economic development, and educational advancement are a few examples of politically as well as intellectually significant enterprises. The crucial impact of this aspect of international relations was recently emphasized by President Johnson at the Smithsonian Institution Bicentennial Celebration in September 1965: "We know today that . . . ideas, not armaments, will shape our lasting prospects for peace; that the conduct of our foreign policy will advance no faster than the curriculum of our classrooms; that the knowledge of our citizens is one treasure which grows only when it is shared."

Despite the remarkable progress made in this field, there remain serious problems concerning objectives, methods, and resources. One aspect that has caused special concern has to do with the impact of United States Government exchange programs overseas where such activities come into the most direct and comprehensive contact with other cultures. This facet of international cultural communication was given special attention in a 1963 report of the United States Advisory Commission on International Educational and Cultural Affairs, chaired by John Gardner, then President of the Carnegie Corporation, now Secretary of Health, Education and Welfare. Stimulated in part by that report—entitled "A Beacon of Hope: The Exchange of Persons Program"—the Hazen Foundation proposed that the Brookings Institution engage in a more thorough analysis of the overseas aspect of United States Government exchange programs. The Institution agreed to undertake this task, with the support of the Hazen Foundation, and was fortunate to enlist the services of Charles Frankel as the author.

During the period when Mr. Frankel wrote this book, he was a Professor of Philosophy at Columbia University, where he had received his doctorate and where he had been teaching since 1939, except for a period of military service from 1942-46. He has had extensive international experience, including visiting professorships at the Universities of Paris and Dublin. His writings include books on *Issues in University Education* and *The Democratic Prospect*. In September 1965, Mr. Frankel was appointed Assistant Secretary of State for Educational and Cultural Affairs. This appointment was made after the present study had been completed; the manuscript was not formally reviewed or approved by the Department of State.

The main objectives of the study are to reexamine the purposes that govern United States Government exchange programs, to describe present institutional arrangements for achieving those objectives, to appraise these practices, and to suggest possible improvements for the future. The focus of the analysis concentrates primarily on civilian programs. Thus it excludes exchange activities conducted by the Department of Defense, although it is recognized that the latter bring more people to the United States for training than any other governmental agency. Because of the study's emphasis on the overseas aspect, it gives little attention to the large variety of related private and public activities within the United States. Furthermore, the focus is on governmental programs. Little is said about private endeavors, although these account for the bulk of cultural exchange.

In gathering material for the study, to supplement his own extensive experience, Mr. Frankel interviewed approximately 300 individuals in twelve countries: Argentina, Austria, Finland, France, Italy, Japan, Morocco, Nigeria, Senegal, the Soviet Union, the United Kingdom, and Uruguay. Both he and the Institution wish to express their gratitude for the exceptional generosity of all those with whom he talked in sharing their knowledge and wisdom. This list includes officials of both the United States and other governments as well as leading figures in many private cultural fields. While it is not feasible to name all of the persons who assisted the author, the Institution and the author would like to cite two key United States Government officials whose cooperation was vital to the success of the enterprise and who were unstintingly helpful in facilitating the study. These are Harry C. McPherson, Jr., former Assistant Secretary of State for Educational and Cultural Affairs, and Arthur W. Hummel, Jr., former Deputy Assistant Secretary of State for Educational and Cultural Affairs.

In line with the usual practice of the Brookings Institution, the author was enabled to consult with an advisory committee composed of the following, with their organizational identification at that time: Edward W. Barrett, Columbia University; Lucius D. Battle, Department of State; Leona Baumgartner, Agency for International Development; Paul J. Braisted, the Hazen Foundation; Frederick Burkhardt, American Council of Learned Societies; Jacob Canter, Department of State; Donald Cook, Department of State; W. Phillips Davison, Council on Foreign Relations; James Echols, United States Information Agency; Harold Enarson, Agency for International Development; George S. Franklin, Council on Foreign Relations; John W. Gardner, Carnegie Corporation; Oscar Handlin, Harvard University; Reed Harris, United States Information Agency; Pendleton Herring, Social Science Research Council; John F. Hilliard, Agency for International Development; John B. Howard, Ford Foundation; Arthur W. Hummel, Jr., Department of State; Richard A. Humphrey, American Council on Education; Walter Johnson, University of Chicago; A. N. Jorgensen, Institute of International Education; Francis Keppel, Department of Health, Education and Welfare; C. W. deKiewiet, American Council on Education; William Marvel, Education and World Affairs; Harry C. McPherson, Jr., Department of State; Hewson A. Ryan, United States Information Agency; Irwin T. Sanders, Ford Foundation; Albert G. Sims, Institute of International Education; John Stalnaker, National Merit Scholarship Corporation; Kenneth Thompson, Rockefeller Foundation; M. H. Trytten, National Academy of Sciences; Rowan A. Wakefield, Agency for International Development; Herman B Wells, Education and World Affairs; Donald Wilson, United States Information Agency; Francis A. Young, Conference Board of Associated Research Councils; Kenneth T. Young, Jr., The Asia Society. Four members of this group, Jacob Canter, James Echols, Richard A. Humphrey, and M. H. Trytten, formed a reading committee that reviewed the final manuscript preliminary to publication.

The author and the Institution wish to express their gratitude to these consultants for their thorough and constructive appraisal of the study. We also wish to thank the Hazen Foundation for its initiation and financial support of the project. H. Field Haviland, Jr., Director of Foreign Policy Studies, was in charge of the project.

The interpretations and conclusions of the author are entirely his responsibility and do not purport to represent the views of the persons consulted, the Hazen Foundation or the trustees, officers, and staff members of the Brookings Institution.

Robert D. Calkins
President

September 1965
Washington, D. C.

Contents

Introduction

THIS IS A STUDY OF American educational and cultural policy abroad—
the neglected aspect, I believe, of United States relations with the rest
of the world. It is neither a historical study nor an examination of administrative organization and procedures. It is a study of principles. Its
purpose is to suggest how to think—or, at any rate, how one man would
think—about American educational and cultural affairs, and particularly
about that small but extremely significant segment of these affairs in
which the federal government has a directing hand. Matters of history
or administration are discussed either to advance the search for controlling principles or to illustrate what such principles might mean
in practice.

The necessity for such a study is great. The current intellectual and
cultural commerce between the United States and other nations has
produced radical changes in international relations. Movies, the mass
media of communication, tourism, publicity, and advertising have altered the character of national cultures and of international discourse.
The activities of universities, foundations, religious groups, fraternal
orders, professional societies, and labor unions have contributed to the
same end. Tensions exist within nations and between nations that
never would have existed were these nations not in such intense cultural communication with one another; new forms of cooperation have
also emerged that undercut traditional political divisions and rivalries
and affect the international balance of power. A major society in the
second half of the twentieth century that fails to develop a systematic
body of thought about this new dimension of international relations

1

is like a seventeenth-century society that failed to give careful attention to the role of commerce overseas.

Yet, although there are today many opinions and many disagreements about how to conduct the educational and cultural relations of the United States with other countries, few of these opinions, and fewer of these disagreements, issue from a careful attempt to examine fundamental principles. In comparison with the sophisticated study and analysis devoted to United States military, economic, or diplomatic policy, little systematic intellectual attention is given to educational and cultural policy. The movement of students, scholars, information, and ideas across frontiers is one of the ancient features of civilized life. One of the proudest boasts of free societies has been that they are hospitable to this movement, and that they believe in the importance of free trade in people and ideas. "We Athenians throw open our city to the world," said Pericles, "and never by alien acts exclude foreigners from any opportunity of learning or observing, even though the eyes of an enemy may occasionally profit by our liberality." But the mere reaffirmation of this ancient principle, noble though it is, is not enough to meet the issues, immediate or long-range, which educational and cultural exchange now pose.

For the character of the movement of people and ideas across borders has altered vastly over the last twenty-five years. The number of people involved is incomparably greater. The social classes and cultural backgrounds from which they are drawn are more varied. The centers of learning to which they go are more numerous, and the places to which they return to use their knowledge are more diversified. Moreover, the framework and objectives of international intellectual and educational relations have changed and grown. The major portion of the support for such relations still comes from private sources of wealth. The majority of foreign students in the United States today, for example, have financed their stay from their own personal or family resources or those of friends. Nevertheless, to a greater extent than ever before, support for educational and cultural exchange is institutional, and is part of an organized program, conducted by corporations, foundations, universities, religious bodies, and international agencies. And national governments have come to play an increasingly large part in international educational and cultural exchange as regulators of the traffic, censors, impresarios, catalytic agents, and sources of support.

Closely connected with these phenomena, there has been an enlargement of the hopes attached to educational and cultural exchange. Old hopes such as the advancement of scholarly inquiry and the broadening of individual horizons and capacities remain, and are, perhaps, stronger than ever. But other purposes and cross-purposes have also entered the picture, and are receiving increasing attention. Educational and cultural exchange is presented as a means to the construction of a peaceful world order. It is held to be indispensable to the economic and social modernization of traditional societies. It is said to be a tool of foreign policy, to be used, like any other tool, to promote the strategic interests of the nation. These enlarged hopes, whether or not they are sound, bespeak something beyond them. They give expression, dimly and obliquely, to what can be described in all sobriety as a change in the relative importance of the different causal factors operative in human history.

Two circumstances in particular have altered the character and significance of international educational and cultural intercourse. The first is the change that has taken place in the nature and sources of the process of technological innovation. In the present century, and particularly in the last quarter of a century, the controlling influence over this process has come to be exercised not by individual engineers, inventors, and entrepreneurs—Nobel, Marconi, Ford—but by organized and subsidized scientific inquiry at fundamental theoretical levels. Although the future practical utility of much basic scientific research cannot be foreseen, it is plain that such research is the major single source of the great tidal changes that are taking place in mankind's relation to nature and in the characteristics of the human scene itself. And this work is carried on around the world by men employing a common professional language, and governed by common procedures and standards of workmanship.

Secondly, there has been a radical change—again, in the main during the last quarter of a century—both in the techniques of rapid communication across great distances, and in the size of the audiences exposed to what is communicated. In the world at large, for the first time since the invention of writing five thousand years ago, more than half of mankind is literate. Probably a third of the human race, furthermore, live in cities, and the tempo of industrialization and urbanization is such that by the end of the century, if present trends continue, less than half of the human beings on the earth will be engaged in agriculture. Nor will peasants be peasants in the classic sense, for not only is agriculture becoming increasingly technological, but roads, radio, and political organization and centralization are breaking down the traditional isolation of the countryside.

These are fundamental shifts in the human condition, and all are taking place at an extraordinary pace in the present generation. These changes in the character of both the more and the less developed societies mean, among other things, that matters that were once considered the business of a few are now considered the business of a great many. They also mean that much larger proportions of the populations in almost all countries have some relationship—or some expectation of a relationship—to the educational system. In the richer, highly developed countries, it is expected that as much as one-third of the population at any given time will be part of the educational system at some level. And in all countries, much larger numbers of people are being brought into closer relation to those traditions in their countries, and to those passing fashions, which bear the honorific label of "culture."

In consequence, scientific institutions, technical information, ideas, and ideologies have today come to constitute much more immediate and significant influences in the history of individual nations and the long-range evolution of mankind's affairs than they have ever been before. Many more people in the world are directly exposed to the products of scholarly and intellectual activity, and many more people have access, and must have access, to the techniques and ideas emanating from the world of learning and higher education. International educational and cultural relations, as a result, can no longer be viewed as limited activities, of interest mainly to the scholarly world. Nor can they be viewed as minor activities either of American universities or the United States Government. They have implications for the destinies of millions, and are among the chief instruments by which men can hope to exercise some control over the destiny of their species. Activities in the field of international education, if they are to be adequate to the tasks to be done, will engage a steadily growing portion of the nation's intellectual and economic resources. It is imperative, therefore, that inherited ideas and ideals be reexamined from the point of view of these new facts, and that the procedures and policies that have emerged in the course of the last twenty-five years be examined from the point of view of their relation to long-range issues and principles. A combination of old clichés and new improvisations will not do.

This applies to private programs, and it obviously applies as well to the programs conducted by the United States Government. The posture and policy of the government with regard to American educational and cultural activities abroad is peculiarly important, even though, in a purely quantitative sense, the government plays a smaller part in these activities than do private organizations. The government's programs are presumably planned with central objectives of national policy in mind. Whether they are planned in this way, they have a special impact because they are presumed to be symbolic of a national commitment— or lack of commitment. The tone of a government program is only too easily identified, by Americans as well as by foreigners, as the American tone; the purposes for which the government uses educational and cultural activities are taken or mistaken for the purposes that American society as a whole assigns to such activities.

Unfortunately, however, the instrumentalities that have been developed by the government for dealing with international educational and cultural affairs have been the consequences, on the whole, less of forethought than of a series of afterthoughts. The introduction of the Fulbright program as part of a program for using counterpart funds abroad is an instructive symbol of the history of educational and cultural policies. Intelligence, ingenuity, and energy have gone into them, and much deep faith and commitment. But these policies have nevertheless usually been attached to other programs with different purposes.

This is not to say that what the United States Government is doing or has done in educational and cultural relations is a failure. On the contrary, the evidence available suggests that the American effort in this field has been one of the most successful of the government's foreign activities.[1] The first large organized efforts in international cultural affairs in the federal government's history can teach Americans a good deal, and not only what to avoid. Many programs, like the

[1] See, for example, *A Beacon of Hope: The Exchange of Persons Program* (Washington: U.S. Advisory Commission on International Educational and Cultural Affairs, 1963).

Fulbright program and the Peace Corps, provide a sound point of departure for what should be done in the future. Indeed, the immensity and delicacy of the tasks performed by such government agencies as the United States Information Agency, the Bureau of Educational and Cultural Affairs of the State Department, and the Agency for International Development must be observed as I have observed them to be fully appreciated. But what exists provides a sound basis for what needs to be done, I believe, only if basic issues can be defined, fundamental purposes sorted out, and priorities established.

In the light of these remarks, I hope it will also be plain that if this study is not primarily addressed to matters of history and administration, still less is it a "report" in the conventional sense of the term. In the preparation of these pages, I have traveled extensively, and have had a chance to talk with scores of people in public and private life, associated with the conduct of American educational and cultural affairs. I have talked with these people in order to be instructed by them, and not to "rate" or "grade" them. No effort is made in these pages to evaluate the success of specific programs in different countries, or to pass judgment on how well the people immediately responsible for their operation are doing their jobs. To do that, after all, requires an answer to a question that is logically prior: What *is* their job? What are the objectives of government-supported educational and cultural activities abroad? This is a question to which there are many answers, but, as yet, too few precise and carefully examined ones.

This does seem the place, however, to record one general judgment. As in any other profession, the people who represent the United States officially in educational and cultural affairs are a mixed crew. My reaction to the fairly large number of them that I have met, however, is that, as a group, they are unusually intelligent, devoted, and self-sacrificing—indeed, almost unduly so. They are better people than the United States, given existing public attitudes toward their work, and given the conditions provided them for doing this work, has a right to expect. Representing the United States Government overseas, particularly in the field of educational, cultural, or scientific affairs, has many intrinsic pleasures, which is the reason those who do the job keep coming back for more. But the rules within which those responsible for educational and cultural relations work, the career patterns open to them, the role assigned to them in the total program of a "Country Team," and the tools made available to them—all these are less than adequate to the important task of educational and cultural representation, and are sometimes incompatible with that task. But tinkering with the nuts and bolts of the bureaucratic organization will not solve the problem. Underlying the existing arrangements are assumptions about the facts and objectives of educational and cultural exchange. Unless these premises and purposes are clarified, most existing difficulties will reappear in any new administrative reorganization.

Accordingly, although the pages that follow contain some definite suggestions for practical reforms, the acceptance or rejection of these suggestions will not be the measure of the success of this study. They are offered as illustrations of a general approach, as ways of indicating what, to my mind, some of its practical implications might be; others, if they agree with this approach, may prefer different ways to put it into action. My fundamental purpose is to affect the terms of discussion, to clarify the principles within which these proposals or any others ought to be discussed. At present, those in charge of American educational and cultural programs are required to give answers to a variety of questions put to them by Congress, by officials in other agencies, and by the public at large. More often than not, their answers are satisfactory; equally often, the questions they are answering are the wrong questions. If these pages can contribute to the asking of better questions about American educational and cultural affairs, they will have accomplished their chief purpose.

For similar reasons, I write not only for those directly concerned with the supervision and execution of government programs or for legislators and specialists in foreign affairs, but for a larger audience—university people, artists, writers, and citizens at large—whose stake in the United States' educational and cultural programs abroad, and whose potential capacity to contribute to these programs, have as yet hardly begun to be recognized. I have therefore included material in the following pages, particularly in the initial chapters, which will be familiar to experts but which is intended to introduce this audience to the nature, functions, and variety of the activities broadly denominated as "educational and cultural affairs." Accurate and enlightened public understanding of these activities is a prerequisite to their success. In the final analysis, the ideas that control the practice of educational and cultural exchange do not belong only to a few specialists but are part of the general atmosphere. They reflect conflicts of interest, gradations of power, and general attitudes toward education, the arts, and the sciences that prevail in American society at large. The review and reassessment of these basic notions is a public affair.

1

The Man in the Middle

EACH YEAR, UNDER THE AUSPICES OF the United States Government, millions of dollars are spent and many thousands of people travel between the United States and other countries in the pursuit of educational objectives or to exchange information and ideas. Books are sent abroad, other books are translated, financial support is given to schools, lecture tours are arranged, experts are dispatched on special missions. Letters requesting information on new techniques of animal husbandry or on admissions procedures of American universities are received, sent—hopefully—to the proper places, and, ultimately, answered. Overseas tours for choruses, orchestras, jazz bands, dramatic groups and basketball teams are sponsored. Exhibitions of paintings and of technological achievements are arranged.

At the request of the United States Government, and under the auspices of one or another of its agencies, American universities send teams of scholars to work with citizens of other countries in economic, scientific, and educational projects. Other Americans go abroad to teach in foreign schools or in American schools overseas. Scholars, students, prominent citizens, government officials, labor leaders, political figures, novelists, engineers, and businessmen from foreign countries come to the United States for brief or extended visits, and are toured, oriented, seminared, lectured, and invited to lecture us.

All this represents a panorama of activities of which many Americans are probably unaware. Like most things human, existing federal programs and instrumentalities for dealing with these manifold activities are the products of an amalgam of deep thought, vague hunches, fac-

9

tional strife, enlightened views of the national interest, compromises—brave, cowardly, or merely ingenious—and grudging acquiescence to overwhelming necessities. Perhaps twenty-five government agencies are engaged in one way or another in educational and cultural relations with other nations.[1] They range from the Department of State to the Department of the Interior, from the United States Information Agency to the National Science Foundation, from the Agency for International Development to the Central Intelligence Agency, and from the Department of Defense to the Peace Corps. The Public Health Service, the Office of Education, and the Atomic Energy Commission are some of the other agencies with important or peripheral responsibilities in this area. Surrounding them are a host of other organizations that are private in their legal status, but which are devoted in part to serving the needs of government programs—for example, the Conference Board of Associated Research Councils and the Institute of International Education.

It is possible to look at these activities from many vantage points. But surely one of the most instructive is to look at them where they initially and finally take shape—where the immediate, detailed decisions are first made, and where the American cultural presence is ultimately perceived and appraised and thought to make a difference in foreign affairs. This is in the field. In each embassy of the United States abroad, there is an officer called the Cultural Affairs Officer or Cultural Attaché. He is the proverbial man in the middle—the man on the spot in both senses of the term. From day to day, no one is closer than he to the scene of action where cultural relations take place not as abstractions planned or recorded on sheets of paper but as immediate, personal events. Although he is not responsible for every activity in the embassy that has a bearing on educational and cultural affairs, no one is more exposed than he to all the pressures and winds of doctrine that play across the field of international educational and cultural affairs. In his daily schedule of activities are mirrored old bureaucratic quarrels and the latest compromise, lingering popular prejudices and carefully considered policies, major decisions of high authority and major indecisions.

A composite portrait of the Cultural Affairs Officer, of the way he

[1] See *Some U.S. Government Agencies Engaged in International Activities* (Bureau of Educational and Cultural Affairs, Department of State, November 1963).

spends his time and the setting in which he works, provides as good an introduction as any to the strange and fascinating territory known as "international educational and cultural affairs." Obviously, there will be some artifice in such a portrait. Cultural Affairs Officers differ as individuals, and do their jobs differently. Moreover, they have different things to do, depending on the countries in which they are serving. The Cultural Affairs Officer I am going to describe is obviously stationed in a smallish country in the southern part of the world. In larger countries he would have more assistance. In richer countries, the presence of larger numbers of American specialists, teachers, and students would complicate his task as well as add to the resources at his command. Yet despite these important differences, there are some significant resemblances among Cultural Affairs Officers and the jobs they have to do. Let us begin, then, by describing a not untypical Cultural Affairs Officer—a gentleman who, in words Gogol used to describe one of his characters, is "neither too fat nor too thin, neither young nor old—a gentleman who is not an Adonis but who is not unprepossessing either."

THE JOB OF THE CULTURAL AFFAIRS OFFICER

What does the Cultural Affairs Officer do from moment to moment? In the morning, when he comes to his office, he will almost certainly find a good deal of correspondence on his desk. Most of it will come from the Bureau of Educational and Cultural Affairs in the State Department (known in "bureaucratese" as "CU") or the United States Information Agency (USIA) in Washington. Some will be for the general information of all people at foreign posts; some will be for the people in his area; some will require action on his part.

He may be informed, for example, that plans are under way to send a college glee club to the country where he is serving—let us call it Evolutia—under the State Department's program of cultural presentations. He will be asked to look into possible travel itineraries, schedules of performances, housing, and opportunities for the members of the glee club to meet the people they ought to meet. He may write back that the glee club, good as it is, should not be sent to Evolutia, since the British Council has just sent the Old Vic through, and the Russians had great success with the Bolshoi Ballet only three months ago. The local audiences, he points out, will inevitably measure the performance of the American group against these standards, and will not make allowance for the fact that the Americans are amateurs. With a touch of weariness he may repeat that Evolutia, inconspicuous though it may seem, is nevertheless unique, and should not be compared with the countries around it. What may work in the larger geographical area in which Evolutia is located will simply not work in Evolutia itself. After writing this reply, our Cultural Affairs Officer begins his inquiries into arrangements for the arrival of the glee club.

There is other news on his desk as well. The word may have arrived that, in response to his request, Washington has found a way to steer toward Evolutia the famed symphony orchestra scheduled to visit the large country next door. The man on the spot thinks how pleasant it will be not to have to explain any longer to his Evolutian friends that the United States Government is not inattentive to their country. There will be other items from Washington requiring his attention. The professor who had been expected to arrive next month to inaugurate a program in American Civilization has had to cancel his plans. On the other hand, three more places have turned up in the United States for Fulbright visiting scholars from Evolutia, and the new librarian he has requested for the American library is finally on her way. There is also a note from the Public Affairs Officer in the embassy asking for his recommendations with regard to the projected tour of the United States by the four members of parliament from Evolutia who have received leadership grants.

Not all his mail, however, comes from Washington or from other people in the Embassy. A student from another country, who had gone to study in one of the Eastern bloc countries, had turned up in the Cultural Attaché's office a month ago and asked for an opportunity to study in the United States. The student's qualifications were ambiguous. He seemed intelligent, but his preparation was uncertain, his English poor, and there was no place for him in the normal exchange program over which the Cultural Affairs Officer had authority since he was not a citizen of Evolutia. Still, it had occurred to the attaché that some American college might be able to find a scholarship for the student, and he had made inquiries. Now he has a letter from a small college on the Pacific Coast asking for more information about the young man. There is another letter, too, from a lady in the mid-West, who is a leader in the "people-to-people" program and is planning a visit to the "sister city" of her home town.

Before getting through his correspondence, however, the Cultural Affairs Officer has to go off to a meeting with the Bi-National Commission in charge of the Fulbright program for exchange of students and scholars. The commission, of which he is chairman, has already drawn up its list of requests for the coming academic year, which has been transmitted through the embassy to the State Department and the Board of Foreign Scholarships in Washington. For this meeting, the principal subject on the agenda is the lack of adequate preparation in English of candidates from Evolutia. The Cultural Affairs Officer reports his hope that a contract teacher of English will be sent to Evolutia next year and will work at the American library. He also reports that the Bi-National Center in Evolutia, which has not been doing an effective job in English-language instruction, is reorganizing its board of directors, and that there are prospects for improvement. The Bi-National Center is an independent organization, supported by private citizens of Evolutia. But the United States has provided the land for the center under the Agricultural Trade Development and Assistance Act of 1954,[2] and the Cultural Affairs Officer is a member of the center's board. He also reports that good things have been heard about a student in the University who may be a candidate for a Fulbright grant in a year or two. He asks the Evolutian members of the commission to find out more about the young man. If the reports continue to be good, perhaps he can make a small sum of money available—say $100—to pay for English lessons for the student at the Bi-National Center.

Following this meeting, the Cultural Affairs Officer goes to meet with the embassy committee, headed by the Ambassador, which decides the allocation of leadership grants. The Political Officer, the Labor Officer, the chief of the Agency for International Development (AID) mission, the Public Affairs Officer, and others all have candidates in mind. The Cultural Affairs Officer reports that the director of the Evolutia National Library, who received a leadership grant the previous year, came home enthusiastic about his visit. He has begun to reform the Library's lending system, and has been telling his friends

[2] P.L. 480, 68 Stat. 454 (1954).

that American libraries, which give readers easy access to books, are like American homes and American life—doors are open, and opportunities are available to those who want them. The story of the librarian makes an impression, and the Cultural Affairs Officer takes the opportunity to push the candidacy of the director of the National Museum. But a new President has just taken office in Evolutia, and the committee decides it would be wiser to give the award to a labor-union leader who is one of the President's close advisers.

When the meeting closes, the Cultural Affairs Officer joins the Public Affairs Officer and the chief of the AID mission in a brief conference with the Ambassador. Farther up the coast, in a neighboring and larger country called Progressia, whose relations with the United States have long been tranquil, there is an American school, supported in part by funds allocated by the Bureau of Educational and Cultural Affairs (CU) in the State Department. Approximately 70 percent of the students in the school are natives of Progressia. The Cultural Affairs Officer, concerned with the difficulties encountered by Evolutian students in adjusting to life in the United States, has urged that the school in Progressia be enlarged so that Evolutian students as well as students from other countries nearby could be sent there to improve their English and to acquire some sense of American ways before going to the United States. The chief of the AID mission, which sends specialists to the United States for training, has seconded this proposal. But CU has reported that it has no more funds to allocate to the school in Progressia, and the AID mission there has not been able to persuade AID in Washington that the school should receive its support.

The Ambassador, however, does not need to have this long, painful story repeated to him. He has been working on the problem, and this morning he has a cheerful word for his officers. The problem has finally worked its way to the desk of the right person in AID in Washington, and the latest news he has received is that there is some prospect for action. But he smiles at his officers and warns them not to think that they have finally won. He reminds them of an old law: "The field is a place where people hope that something will happen in Washington. Washington is a place where people fear that something will happen in the field."

The Cultural Affairs Officer then brings up two other matters that emerged from the conferences he had the preceding day at the Ministry of Education and the Ministry of Culture. At the Ministry of Education, the permanent under-secretary had expressed concern that the selection of people for specialist and leadership grants was made entirely by the embassy, and had suggested that his government desired the opportunity to participate in the selection process. The Cultural Affairs Officer tells the Ambassador that he agreed to carry this report back to him, but had added the comment that he was not optimistic that a change in the selection procedure would be made.

At the Ministry of Culture, he goes on to report, the discussion had revolved around the exchange of presentations in the performing arts. The Evolutians had expressed great satisfaction at the reception accorded the Evolutian folk-dance group that had toured the United States the previous year, and wondered about the possibility of a follow-up. The Cultural Affairs Officer, in supporting the idea, goes on to remark to the Ambassador that, in his view, good will toward the United States and a favorable image of its culture would perhaps be better promoted in Evolutia by giving Americans the chance to applaud Evolutians in the States than by sending cultural presentations to Evolutia. The Ambassador expresses interest, and a meeting is scheduled with him and the Public Affairs Officer for the following week to discuss the general problem of "reverse flow" more fully.

After this brief conference, the Cultural Affairs Officer drives to the airport to greet Evolutia's leading ballerina, who is returning from a tour of the United States, and takes her to the small lunch in her honor which he has arranged. (It is late in the fiscal year, and the representation funds at his disposal have been used up. He pays for the lunch out of his own pocket.)

When the Cultural Attaché returns to his office, he has a difficult twenty minutes with one of the local employees in his office, whose position has been cut from the budget next year, and whom he has to inform of this decision. The Cultural Attaché then turns to work on a draft of the report he is preparing, at Washington's request, on current attitudes toward the educational exchange program of former grantees from Evolutia. He is interrupted, however, by a young man with a complaint. On his own initiative, the young man reports, he had written the admissions office of what he thought to be a first-rate university in the United States; now, after some months, he finds that he had merely been in contact with an agricultural college, and he feels deceived, indignant, and snubbed. The Cultural Attaché does his best to suggest to his visitor that he was not wrong in the first place, and that he has really been in touch with a first-rate institution, which happens to have an agricultural school. Then he asks, a bit hesitantly, whether the young man, who comes from the countryside, might not find the scientific study of agriculture interesting. This leads to a long, personal discussion with the visitor, who turns out to be a charming and disarming fellow, and the report to Washington is postponed once more.

After his visitor leaves, the Cultural Affairs Officer receives a telephone call from his superior, the Public Affairs Officer in the embassy, who wishes to know if he has a copy of the informal remarks he plans to make the next evening at the resort in the mountains where the summer concert season has opened, and a special evening devoted to American composers is scheduled. He promises to send off a copy, and turns back to his typewriter when the telephone rings again. It is the Ambassador's wife, asking him for advice. The new president's daughter is about to leave for a vacation in New York, and it would be good if she had a book about the United States to read on the plane. Of course, the young lady's English is limited. Is there a good, short book in Evolutian, or perhaps in Progressian? And if so, where could it be obtained? Happily, the Cultural Affairs Officer has given extensive study to the question, for he has spent much time reviewing the materials in the American library. He has, in fact, been instrumental in having just the right book translated into Evolutian, and he tells the Ambassador's wife that he will get her a copy. After this, he makes an effort to get on with the writing of his report. But he has to stop in order to describe his work to a visitor from the States who is doing a study of educational and cultural affairs.

At six o'clock, a little late for his appointment, he drives out to the university, where he is joining half a dozen Evolutian students for an informal discussion of Faulkner. On the way out, he tries to recover the ideas on Faulkner which he once had when he was an instructor in English, but he suspects that the conversation will not stay on Faulkner long. As events turn out, he is right. He does not leave his friends until midnight. The conversation has ranged over race relations in the United States, the socialist movement in Evolutia, the perennial backwardness of Progressia, and the fate of hot jazz.

The next morning the Cultural Affairs Officer is on the road early, for he wishes to stop off, on his way to the mountains, at two provincial schools where teachers of English are being selected for special training in the United States. He also hopes to make a stop at the regional Cultural Center established by the Evolutian government, where there is a small collection of Americana to which his office has contributed. The Director of the Center and his assistant are both genial and cultivated men who speak English well and have a lively and friendly interest in the United States although neither has ever been in the country. On a number of occasions, they have complained to him that their authority, when they speak in their community about things American, is questioned, while the opinions of less well-informed people —labor leaders, local politicians, newspaper editors—are given greater credence. The reason, so they say, is that the latter have been to the United States (often at the expense of the United States Government) while they have not. They believe that this state of affairs undermines their authority as cultural leaders, and adversely affects their utility to American cultural programs. The Cultural Attaché will have to tell them that he has mentioned their problem to his colleagues at the embassy, and that his colleagues were sympathetic and hoped that something could eventually be done. But for the present. . . .

These, of course, are just two days in the job of one man. On other days, he might have other things to do. For one thing, many peripheral chores frequently come his way. More than his colleagues at the same level in the embassy, a Cultural Attaché is likely to be called upon by the Ambassador to represent the United States on ceremonial occasions. On his calendar, too, are receptions at other embassies, first nights at the theater, meetings of the literary club, and staff conferences about the housing for American Fulbright students. On many days as well, he, or a member of his staff, will have to drive to the airport to greet some visiting American whose visit is thought to have an educational or cultural aspect. Often it is the Cultural Affairs Officer, or one of his assistants, who has taken care of the visitor's lodgings and schedule of appointments, even when the visitor has not come on official business. Often, too, there are visitors, official and unofficial, whose missions have nothing explicitly to do with education and culture, but who wish to advance their own education and culture by taking in the local scenery. As likely as not, it is the Cultural Attaché who will be asked to provide the personally guided tour. After all, is he not the man in the embassy whose job it is to know the local culture best?

THE WORKING CONDITIONS OF THE CULTURAL AFFAIRS OFFICER

Needless to say, if the Cultural Affairs Officer were in a country other than Evolutia, his job would in many respects be different. In a country with a large and developed higher educational system, a much greater part of his attention would probably be given to making close contacts with scholars, and to facilitating contacts between American scholars and their colleagues in the host country. In a country where the study of English as a secondary language is compulsory, he would not be beating the bushes for teachers of English, but his task would be the equally complicated one of trying to ensure that the teachers that existed had sufficient opportunity to hear English spoken by a native speaker. In a country whose geographical position or historical lustre made it a center for international scholarly meetings and for students from many lands, part of his energies might have to be devoted not simply to relations with the host country, but to multinational relations. As sometimes happens in exceptional cases, if he were a man with a reputation of his own as a scholar, artist, or intellectual, he might decide to leave administration to his subordinates and to act, in the main, as a member of the intellectual community in the host country, writing, lecturing, contributing to the journals, and establishing his own place on the intellectual and cultural scene.

Moreover, depending on the size of the country to which he is accredited and on other factors such as the magnitude of the exchange program and the availability of qualified people, a Cultural Affairs Officer will have more or less assistance in performing the variety of tasks that are likely to fall within his domain. In large posts, he may have two or three officers working under his direction. In such countries, a Cultural Affairs Officer will be able to be more selective in the tasks he himself chooses to perform. In other missions, he alone may be on the job. In all posts, large or small, however, he invariably depends on local employees. Often, many of these people have been involved in the educational and cultural programs of the embassy for a much longer period than he; equally often, the success of the Cultural Affairs Officer's efforts can be affected by the calibre and sense of dedication of these people.

Despite the variations in the amount and quality of the help Cultural Affairs Officers receive, however, one fact stands out—at any rate as far as the countries I have visited are concerned. Some Cultural Affairs Officers have expressed the need for more people to do the central job. Others have said that they would be content simply to have more assistance with the clerical chores that surround the job. But at no post was the Cultural Affairs Officer satisfied that he had enough time to do his job as he should or enough people to help him.

"Complaint" is not the word to use to describe these reactions of Cultural Affairs Officers to their working conditions. Most of those with whom I have talked accept their job with an open-eyed and cheerful recognition both of its dimensions and of the inadequacy of the resources that will be made available to them. Nevertheless, most of them are acutely aware that their offices are understaffed. Most of them are also uncomfortable with the allocation of their time forced on them by the paperwork and other routines of the embassy. They feel that they spend less time than they should away from their desks, where the most important tasks of cultural liaison are performed. To be sure, the feeling that there are not enough hours in the day and not enough people to do the job is not uncommon to men who take their positions seriously. The description that has been given of a Cultural Affairs Officer's job may suggest, however, that in his case there is more than the normal justification for such a feeling.

THE "COMPLEAT" CULTURAL AFFAIRS OFFICER

Apart from the differences in the assistance he receives, the central tasks of the Cultural Affairs Officer have surprising constancy from one country to another. As previously noted, there may be variations, and sometimes significant ones, in the job a Cultural Affairs Officer must do. On the whole, however, the difference in the job between country and country or region and region is not so much in the tasks to be done as in the relative priority to be assigned to them and the way one goes about performing them. In Western Europe as in Evolutia, a Cultural Attaché ought to be aware of the direction of growth and of the emerging needs of the host country's educational system. In Evolutia as in Western Europe, he should be alert to ways in which American scholarship and culture might benefit from exchanges. And no matter where he is, his job calls for him to be a diplomat and negotiator, an educational planner and administrator, a middleman between two cultures, and a reasonably attractive embodiment of the American cultural presence.

It is, indeed, an assignment that calls for an unusual combination of qualities. As the description of two days in the life of a normally competent, normally harassed Cultural Affairs Officer may suggest, the ideal or "compleat" Cultural Affairs Officer would be a protean character. He would be an intellectual with gregarious instincts; a warm-hearted communicator between two cultures and yet a hard-headed negotiator; an administrator of a large staff and program who keeps his staff and program in hand while he spends most of his time out of his office; a faithful bureaucrat who nevertheless can deal with the temperamental idiosyncrasies of professors, musicians, athletes, and VIP's. In short, he would be a man of parts with the tastes of an aristocrat, the patience of a saint, and the constitution of a shotputter. If he can manage it, he should also be a man who has a beautiful and charming wife who loves his job as much as he does, speaks the language of the country as well as he, and has inherited a comfortable sum of money so that she can supply what his representation fund lacks.

THE MEN WHO DO THE JOB

As it will not be surprising to report, candidates for the position of Cultural Affairs Officer who possess all these qualities are not invariably available. Nevertheless, it is interesting, against this sketch of the ideal Cultural Attaché, to look at a sample of the people who are serving in these posts around the world. What are their education and background? What are their prospects within the USIA? To which career service are they attached? How do they compare in these respects with their fellows in USIA missions? The following statistics, though incomplete, are suggestive. They are based on a study of 30 Cultural

Affairs Officers, 25 Information Officers, and 36 Public Affairs Officers whose files were made available. They are roughly one-third of the officers serving in these posts around the world at the end of 1964.

For the 30 Cultural Affairs Officers, the mean average age at which their appointment to the full rank of Cultural Affairs Officer was received is 45.1, while the median age is 43. In comparison, their opposite numbers, the Information Officers, who have the same rank in a USIA mission, [3] are somewhat younger, their average age being 44.4, and their median age 38. Interestingly enough, the 36 Public Affairs Officers studied, although they occupy higher ranks in the administrative echelon, are not significantly different from the Cultural Affairs Officers in terms of the ages at which they moved to their present rank. The average age is 44.7, the median age 43.

In educational backgrounds and job experience, the differences between the three groups are more striking. Among the 30 Cultural Affairs Officers, 21, or 70 percent, have degrees higher than the Bachelor's, and 12 have Ph.D's. Among the 25 Information Officers, only 3 have Master's degrees, and none has a Doctorate. The 36 Public Affairs Officers include 12 (33 percent) who have degrees higher than the Bachelor's, and among these two have Ph.D.'s. Nineteen of the Cultural Affairs Officers held academic positions before entering the foreign service; others had experience in administration, journalism, public relations or the military services. Eighteen of the 25 Information Officers, in contrast, worked previously in journalism, public relations, or mass communications; the others had administrative or military experience. Among the 36 Public Affairs Officers, 23 have backgrounds in journalism, the mass media or public relations; 4 had academic or research experience before entering USIA; 3 had both journalistic and academic experience.

Perhaps the most significant figure, however, is that among the 36 Public Affairs Officers in the sample studied, only 3 had been Cultural Affairs Officers. All but one of the rest came from service as information or media officers. A USIA memorandum of April 29, 1964, entitled *Public Affairs Officers and Deputy Public Affairs Officers who are also qualified Cultural Affairs Officers*, gives a different picture, but not a substantially different one. Out of a total of 106 officers canvassed, 38

[3] See the Appendix for the organization chart of a USIA mission.

are reported as "qualified Cultural Affairs Officers." This phrase, however, is used broadly. It signifies that the officers in question have had two or more years of experience either in cultural affairs overseas or in the "cultural" aspects of USIA programs in Washington—for example, libraries, book translations, and subsidies, or preparation of exhibits. Even in these broad terms, only a little more than one-third of the Public Affairs Officers qualify as Cultural Affairs Officers. On the whole, it does not appear that experience or competence as a Cultural Affairs Officer is the most favorable route to advancement within the USIA. Although Cultural Affairs Officers are not notably disadvantaged with regard to advancement in Foreign Service grade and salary, they are at a disadvantage so far as advancement to positions of status and top responsibility are concerned. This is the more noteworthy since Cultural Affairs Officers as a group are more highly educated and somewhat older than their opposite numbers, the Information Officers.

One or two other figures will complete this brief sketch of the Cultural Affairs Officer. It is interesting—and it may provide a clue to recruitment possibilities—to note that of the 30 Cultural Affairs Officers in the sample, 8 were born abroad, 2 of these being naturalized United States citizens. (Only 2 of the 25 Information Officers were born abroad, while 9 of the 36 Public Affairs Officers fall into this category.) Twelve of the Cultural Affairs Officers studied abroad. Almost all appear to know at least one foreign language; approximately half show competence in two or more.

A significant fact about the Cultural Affairs Officers does not appear, however, from a recital of cold statistics. The study of their files shows that they have been drawn, in the main, from two categories. One category, by far the smaller, is the senior academic figure. In the sample of 30 Cultural Affairs Officers studied, 6 are men who took the position after many years in academic life, and without previous experience in USIA. Four were over 55 when they did so, the other two were in their forties. Men in this category who serve as Cultural Affairs Officers often have distinguished reputations in their professional fields, and bring the prestige of their names to their positions.

By far the larger category of Cultural Affairs Officers, however, comes from what is probably, if the future is being considered, an atypical generation. Again and again, there appears in the career-history of those studied a sharp tangential change of direction—a movement from academic life to international affairs. The occasion appears to have been a period of service in military intelligence, administration, or education, or in the Office of War Information. In brief, it appears that most of the men serving as Cultural Affairs Officers today might not have been in such work were it not for their war experiences. To replace this generation, USIA is proceeding on the policy of bringing in new people at the bottom and training them. Whether this policy will produce as good results as the windfall after World War II remains to be seen. It is plain, in any case, that the calibre of the Cultural Affairs Officer of the future cannot safely be predicted by observing the calibre of those presently serving in the post. Looking ahead, the problem of recruiting and training Cultural Affairs Officers, and of designing an attractive career for them, is bound to require increasing attention.

2

Circles Within Circles

THE CONDUCT OF OFFICIAL United States educational and cultural activities abroad cannot be understood by looking at the Cultural Affairs Officer alone. He stands at the center of a field on which different forces converge, and what he does is intelligible only if one understands the nature of these forces. The formation and implementation of American educational and cultural programs overseas are influenced by (1) the immediate administrative setting in which the Cultural Attaché does his job; (2) the relation between his activities and those of other embassy officials, or of other United States Government missions in the host country; (3) the intimate and decisive interconnection between the public and private sectors in the conduct of educational and cultural programs; (4) the audiences, in the host country and in the United States, whose attitudes and reactions play a crucial role in determining what is done and what success is achieved. The first two of these are considered in this chapter. In the succeeding two chapters the others will be discussed.

THE IMMEDIATE ADMINISTRATIVE SETTING

The administrative setting in which the Cultural Affairs Officer does his job is not the same as that of most of his colleagues in the embassy. He stands at the end of two channels of communication, two lines of authority. He is a member of the United States Information Agency mission. His immediate superior in the embassy is the Public Affairs

Officer, who is the head of the USIA mission in the country. At the same time, however, the Cultural Affairs Officer reports not only to USIA but also to the Bureau of Educational and Cultural Affairs in the Department of State. To be sure, the Public Affairs Officer, or any other officer handling educational and cultural exchanges, may also be in communication with CU. Nevertheless, what is incidental to the jobs of his colleagues in the USIA mission is central to the job of the Cultural Affairs Officer. The very essence of his job is that he must look in two directions.

The duality in the Cultural Affairs Officer's position is also reflected in the sources of the services and support he receives. If he wishes to encourage a program of American studies in the universities, for example, he will ask the Bureau of Educational and Cultural Affairs to find a suitable visiting lecturer; but he will turn to the Cultural Operations Division of the USIA's Information Center Service for help in procuring books, visual materials, maps, and library equipment. He will turn to the appropriate regional and country desks in both CU and USIA for advice and guidance in establishing such a program.

Behind this state of affairs lies the story of the federal government's operations and improvisations in the field of international educational, cultural, and information programs. Until the late 1930's, most efforts to facilitate and promote international educational and cultural exchange had been carried on in the United States by universities, foundations, and religious groups. The federal government had engaged in such activities only tangentially. Congress, for example, had authorized the Smithsonian Institution to make suitable arrangements for the export of literary and scientific materials.[1]

It was not until 1938, however, and largely in response to Nazi and Fascist efforts to win support in Latin America, that a formal agency was created by the federal government specifically for the purpose of conducting educational and cultural relations. This was the Division of Cultural Relations, established in the State Department, following the signing, at Buenos Aires in 1937, of the Convention for the Promotion

---

[1] In the early years of the century, the government had also taken a small but significant action that is interesting because it foreshadowed American actions that were to come. After the Boxer Rebellion, the indemnities to be paid by China to the United States were set apart, by agreement between the Chinese and United States governments, to assist Chinese students.

of Inter-American Cultural Activities. In 1941, the post of "Cultural Relations Officer" was created.

During the war years, the propaganda and cultural activities of the United States Government were conducted largely under the auspices of the Office of War Information. After the war, a series of administrative changes took place. In 1946, an Office of International Information and Cultural Affairs was established in the State Department, to be replaced the next year, after a reduction in the appropriations voted by Congress, by an Office of International Information and Educational Exchange. This office had the responsibility for administering both the Fulbright Act and a reduced information program. In the next year, after the passing of the Smith-Mundt Act, which further formalized and extended the government's interest in educational and cultural exchange, this office was divided into two parts, an Office of International Information, and an Office of Educational Exchange, and both were placed under the direction of an Assistant Secretary of State for Public Affairs. In 1952, this action was reversed, and, once again, a single agency, the International Information Administration, was established. It remained within the Department of State.

In 1953, after the Eisenhower Administration came to power, the place to be assigned to overseas informational, educational, and cultural activities within the general structure of the federal government was reexamined. At first, conflicting recommendations were made, but finally the recommendation prevailed that an independent information agency should be established outside the Department of State. To a large extent, the triumph of this point of view, which was advocated by the United States Advisory Commission on Information, seems to have been due to the fact that Secretary of State John Foster Dulles also favored it, wishing as he did to free the Department of State from responsibility for operations in the field other than those directly related to the conduct of diplomacy in the traditional sense.

However, a subcommittee of the Senate Foreign Relations Committee, headed by Senator Bourke Hickenlooper, after considering the proposed reorganization, recommended that educational exchange should not be a function of the new information agency, but should remain the responsibility of the Department of State. In making this recommendation, the members of the subcommittee had two considerations in mind. They feared that the educational exchange program would be downgraded if it were removed from the State Department, and they wished to keep educational and cultural affairs clearly separated from propaganda activities. At the hearings conducted by the subcommittee, Senator J. W. Fulbright said, "If you seek to coordinate them [the Board of Foreign Scholarships, which has final responsibility for the Fulbright program] in any degree—make them subordinate or direct them as a part of a government propaganda agency—I think by that act you will have destroyed their principal usefulness, and destroyed their incentive to function." Senator Fulbright went on to mention the binational commissions overseas and the prominent citizens of cooperating countries serving on them, and said, "I do not for a minute believe that they would become a part of any . . . information organization that would coordinate them and direct them as to what to do." [2] On May 9, 1953, Senator Hickenlooper, as Chairman of the Committee, sent to the President a Senate resolution expressing the view that educational exchange programs should remain in the Department of State.[3]

In consequence, in June 1953, the United States Information Agency was established outside the Department of State, but the State Department, through the International Educational Exchange Service, Bureau of Public Affairs, continued to exercise authority over educational and cultural relations. This state of affairs has persisted to the present, with one major change. The Kennedy Administration, in 1961, raised the organizational status of educational and cultural affairs, and further signalized their separation from information activities, by appointing an Assistant Secretary of State for Educational and Cultural Affairs.[4]

[2] *Overseas Information Programs of United States,* Hearings before the Senate Committee on Foreign Relations, 83 Cong., 1 sess., Pt. 2 (1953), p. 864.

[3] Reprinted in the final report of the committee, *Overseas Information Programs of United States,* S. Rept. 406, 83 Cong., 1 sess. (1953).

[4] For more complete accounts of these events see George N. Shuster, "The Nature and Development of United States Cultural Relations," in Robert Blum, ed., *Cultural Affairs and Foreign Relations,* The American Assembly, Columbia University (Prentice-Hall, 1963); *The U.S. Ideological Effort: Government Agencies and Programs* (Study prepared by the Legislative Reference Service, Library of Congress, for the Subcommittee on International Organizations and Movements of the House Committee on Foreign Affairs, Jan. 3, 1964); and Charles A. Thomson and Walter H. C. Laves, *Cultural Relations and U.S. Foreign Policy* (Indiana University Press, 1963). Ruth McMurry and Muna Lee, *The Cultural Approach—Another Way in International Relations* (University of North Carolina Press, 1947) recounts the story up to 1946.

These various reforms, however, have left paradoxes, or what appear to be paradoxes, in their wake. In particular, the decision to separate education from information, and CU from USIA, left a number of practical questions unanswered, including the most practical question of all—where the staff to operate a separate educational and cultural exchange program in the field would come from. As a consequence, despite the formal separation of CU from USIA in Washington, the staffs and the activities of the two agencies have remained unified in the field. Under an agreement with the State Department, USIA has continued to be responsible for educational and cultural as well as information activities overseas, and has continued to be the employer of the people who administer government exchange programs in the field. USIA's mandate, in fact, is extremely broad. A memorandum from President Kennedy to the Director of USIA, dated January 23, 1963, makes the USIA missions overseas responsible for the conduct of public information, public relations, and cultural activities for every agency of the United States Government except the Defense Department. Key positions in CU in Washington are also often filled by USIA officers.

In sum, the separation of CU from USIA in Washington apparently exemplifies the principle that educational and cultural activities should be kept separate from propaganda activities. The position of the Cultural Affairs Officer as a member of the USIA mission in the field appears to exemplify the opposite principle. In 1963, the United States Advisory Commission on International Educational and Cultural Affairs, in its report to Congress, commented on this problem:

> From many diverse sources in our study the well-worn question has come up repeatedly—whether field supervision by USIA of the Cultural Affairs Officer and of the cultural and educational program as a whole is in the best long-term interests of the program. We believe that this whole question of the management of the exchange program in the field under the aegis of USIA, and of the quality and character of personnel required, needs considerable study.[5]

Yet the ambiguous position of the Cultural Affairs Officer with his responsibilities to two hierarchies is probably not the most striking feature of the present administrative structure. Even more striking is the

[5] *A Beacon of Hope: The Exchange of Persons Program* (Washington: U.S. Advisory Commission on International Educational and Cultural Affairs, 1963), p. 47.

fact that the USIA, an agency whose universally accepted mission is to promote the foreign policy of the administration, is outside the State Department, while educational and cultural affairs, whose character and significance might be thought to transcend the day-to-day pressures that bear on foreign policy, are inside the State Department.[6] On paper if not in fact, the international propaganda activities of the United States Government enjoy more administrative autonomy than the government's international educational and cultural activities. It is quite possible, of course, that this arrangement represents the most practical solution possible of a complex problem. Although it is the product of a series of ad hoc compromises—or perhaps precisely because it is the product of such compromises—it may be an effective arrangement. But that there is an appearance of paradox is unquestionable.

Nevertheless, it is important not to exaggerate the consequences from the standpoint of administrative efficiency of these apparently complex administrative arrangements. In the field, there is rarely much ambiguity about the Cultural Affairs Officer's position. He is a member of the USIA mission, a career officer of that organization working under the direction of the Public Affairs Officer. Within that setting, furthermore, established working principles define his responsibilities fairly sharply. Such principles are illustrated in the relation between the Information Officer and the Cultural Affairs Officer, whose jobs, in principle, might overlap at various points. The Information Officer does not concern himself exclusively with political or diplomatic news. He turns out magazines or puts together radio programs dealing not simply with current events but with such subjects as the political institutions of the United States, higher education, community musical activities, the work of American poets, or developments in scientific research. The distinction between his job and that of the Cultural Affairs Officer is not that one deals with "cultural" matters while the other never does. It is a difference in the techniques they use. The Information Officer employs the so-called "fast media" of communication—for example, magazines and television—which are presumed to achieve their impact quickly; the

---

[6] With the exception of administration, the Bureau of Educational and Cultural Affairs is the largest single bureau in the department in terms of budget and the number of people working for it.

Cultural Affairs Officer calls on the so-called "slow media"—teachers, students, and books—whose work is accomplished more slowly.

This practical division between "fast" and "slow" media is useful in preventing conflicts of authority; at the same time, the close association of the Information Officer and the Cultural Affairs Officer in the same section of the embassy permits them to assist each other's efforts closely. A similar practical division of labor between USIA and CU in Washington has been worked out. CU deals with that part of educational and cultural exchange that involves *persons,* while USIA handles *things* —for example, libraries, books and book translations, films, tapes.

By far the most important instrument for keeping potential difficulties under control, however, is the principle that the Ambassador, as head of the "country team," is the official to whom all parties report. He is expected to coordinate and unify different programs and chains of command. The coordination of USIA activities and the activities of the Bureau of Educational and Cultural Affairs—assuming coordination is what is wanted—is in fact not as difficult a job in the field, where all these activities take place under a single commander, as it is in Washington, where the agencies are large and separate. Difficulties are created by the double lines of authority that converge on the Cultural Attaché, but a divided command and administrative inefficiency, although they occur, are not outstanding among them.

THE AMBIGUOUS POSITION OF THE
CULTURAL AFFAIRS OFFICER

Other problems, however, are created by these arrangements. One is that the Cultural Affairs Officer usually has a different background than most of his colleagues in the USIA mission, whose experience, for the most part, has been in journalism and the mass media. Another closely connected problem is that the Cultural Affairs Officer is likely to feel that the prospects for his promotion to a higher level are less good than those of his colleagues, and that if he is advanced, he will have to pay a price by cutting down or altogether forsaking activities that are at the center of his interest. That there is an objective basis for this feeling is suggested by the statistics given in the last chapter.

Probably the greatest cost of existing arrangements from the point of view of personnel policy, however, is that they tend to discourage qualified people from entering the field of cultural affairs. No one, of course, can say how large the loss of good candidates is, but in a field in which people with the requisite talents are bound to be in short supply, the loss surely is serious. There can be little question that individuals with an appropriate background in scholarship, literature, the arts, or educational administration are likely to be wary of cutting the lines to their own profession, and entering a setting dominated by journalists, publicists, and specialists in the mass media. There is even less question that top-flight men with established reputations will hesitate to take a position that is likely to seem to them to be fairly low on the totem pole. Given the capacities and background required by the position of Cultural Affairs Officer, and given the importance and delicacy of the duties attached to the position, it is not high enough in the chain of command. There are only one or two cases in which Cultural Attachés have been given rank and authority commensurate with their responsibilities.

Against all this, it should be recorded that many Cultural Affairs Officers would not willingly trade their position, which they regard as the most agreeable and interesting in the embassy, for a position that carries more prestige and authority. The problems that have been mentioned—of recruitment, promotion, and administrative authority—are grave, but they are not the gravest problems affecting the conduct of educational and cultural affairs abroad. The gravest problems have to do with the effect of the administrative and institutional environment in which the Cultural Affairs Officer does his job, on other matters, such as the definition of his task, the expectations that are entertained concerning what he is supposed to accomplish, and the criteria that are employed in judging his performance. Most Cultural Affairs Officers with whom I have talked do not complain that they are victims of divided counsels or administrative inefficiency. They do not complain, that is to say, that their position is confusing because they are members of two teams, CU and USIA. They complain that they are members of the wrong team or of no team at all—that what they are doing is either force-fitted to other people's programs and goals, or is regarded as a mere grace note to embassy activity.

From this point of view, there are four principal defects of existing arrangements. The first is that the USIA mission has definitive objectives from year to year, objectives that are geared tightly to the embassy's country plan. But the Cultural Affairs Officer's program has objectives that cannot be measured on a year-to-year basis, and the success of the activities he conducts is not susceptible to measurement by the same standards as those that may appropriately be applied to information programs. This conflict between the Cultural Affairs Officer's *long-term* objectives and the *short-term* objectives central to the USIA mission's work is fundamental. If an effort is made to fit the Cultural Attaché's programs to the short-term objectives of the information program, the cultural programs are distorted. If it is recognized that they should not be measured by the same standards as those applicable to an information program, the Cultural Attaché occupies a private place off by himself in the USIA mission and he not infrequently pulls up the rear in the procession.

A second problem, which is also a product of the existing administrative arrangements, is that a major function of cultural relations tends to be ignored. The principal purpose of a USIA mission is to inform the officials and the citizens of the host country. But effective cultural relations depend on a two-way process. The Cultural Affairs Officer and all those involved in his program must listen as well as talk; they must seek to interpret the foreign culture to Americans and not only American culture to foreigners. Admitting that a good Information Officer also knows how to listen, there is, or should be, a different tone and emphasis in the work of the Cultural Affairs Officer. Within the setting of a USIA mission, this tone and emphasis can easily be submerged.

Indeed, one of the most important potential functions of the Cultural Attaché may be ignored. Due to the nature of his work, he is often better informed than anyone else in the embassy about currents of opinion in intellectual, artistic, and student circles, and is capable of making a significant contribution as a reporter and analyst. In present circumstances, he does little or nothing of this.

A third and immensely important problem is that a USIA mission provides a peculiar and comparatively narrow angle of vision from which to see the educational needs either of a host country or of the United States. The Cultural Affairs Officer, if he can claim to have anything that resembles a coherent program, is engaged in a program of educational planning. But such educational planning, if it takes place at all, is likely to be a subordinate element in the program of a USIA mission. An elementary example is the use to which, in many embassies, the program of leader and specialist grants is put. It is unquestionable that the Ambassador and the Public Affairs Officer should have grants at their disposal that they can use to promote the work of the embassy. Such grants for tactical political purposes do not become educational or cultural grants, however, simply because they come from the budget of the Bureau of Educational and Cultural Affairs. Necessary and desirable though they may be, they should be considered in their own setting and have their own separate budget. For they may have little to do with the central objectives of a program of educational and cultural cooperation.

But the fourth and largest problem comes from the mixing of two distinct objectives, one of which can only do harm to the other. The relation of "information" and "propaganda" on the one side to "education" and "culture" on the other will be explored in greater depth later. For the moment, it is enough to point out that an information program tends to embarrass and compromise an educational and cultural program when it is too closely and visibly associated with it. For the central commitment of an information program is quite properly to the United States foreign policy of the moment, accepted as given, while the commitment of an educational and cultural program is to open-ended inquiry, the free exchange of opinions, and the search for a common ground for mutual understanding.

Undoubtedly, an educational and cultural program, particularly if it seems to have no direct propagandistic purpose, contributes to the effectiveness of an information program. Speaking before a Senate subcommittee in 1953, Robert L. Johnson, head of the International Information Agency, remarked that educational exchanges were the "hard core" of the information program, and observed that educational and cultural exchange gives an information program "greater strength, greater respectability and greater credibility." [7] The difficulty with this view, however, is that an information program borrows from the credit

[7] Minutes of Advisory Commission on Educational Exchange, Dec. 4, 5, 1953. This letter and other valuable material were presented at the hearing before a Subcommittee of the Senate Committee on Foreign Relations. See: *Overseas Information Programs of the United States*, 83 Cong., 1 sess., Pt. 2, pp. 863, 1046.

of an educational and cultural program, but it gives nothing back. Each time it draws on the reservoir of credit built up by the educational and cultural program, it tends to deplete that reservoir. The utility of an American library is compromised when, as is generally the case, it is composed of books that are clearly pre-selected to deliver a message. The people who visit the library are not so naive that they do not realize the character of the institution they are visiting. The utility of the library is doubly compromised when, as is often literally and always figuratively the case, mimeograph machines on the floor above are turning out statements defending the most recent action of the United States in foreign affairs.

Curiously enough, judging from the interviews I have conducted, it is not the Cultural Affairs Officer but, more usually, the Public Affairs Officer who is the principal sufferer from this mixture of functions. Most Public Affairs Officers regard themselves not simply as the chief information officer of the Embassy but as the chief cultural officer. Given existing arrangements, this is as it should be. But for many of these officers, the effort to carry on both functions at the same time is difficult and often self-defeating. The capital an officer builds up in performing the tasks of cultural liaison, he loses in performing the tasks of an advocate. Those Public Affairs Officers who have had previous service as Cultural Affairs Officers are particularly sensitive to this dilemma.

THE VARIETY OF GOVERNMENT PROGRAMS

The conduct of educational and cultural programs overseas is also affected by the fact that many of these programs fall outside the area of responsibility of either CU or USIA. A description of all the ways in which different agencies of the federal government may be represented in educational and cultural activities overseas would not be possible without making this study unduly long. But some sense of the variety and complexity of these programs can be transmitted by a consideration of some of the more notable patterns of activity.

In the underdeveloped countries, the Agency for International Development and the Peace Corps are both usually represented. AID sends people to the United States (or to other places) for short or long periods of training, and brings teachers, specialists, and sometimes entire teams of experts to host countries. Where it is engaged in educational assistance projects, it generally has an Education Officer attached to its mission. Over all, AID reaches more people through its education and training programs than does CU or USIA. Generally speaking, too, wherever the Peace Corps is represented, it usually has more Americans on the scene under its auspices than are present under the auspices of exchange programs for which the Cultural Affairs Officer has responsibility.

In the developed countries, although AID and the Peace Corps are not represented, other federal agencies are likely to have large educational or cultural programs. Conspicuous examples are the Atomic Energy Commission and the National Science Foundation. (These agencies may also be represented in underdeveloped countries.) In Japan, for example, cooperative research programs sponsored by the National Science Foundation probably involve a larger number of individuals, Americans and Japanese, than does the Fulbright program. In Japan, too, many American students, present under the terms of the National Defense Education Act, have stipends larger than those of ordinary Fulbright grantees, and their presence in the country is not directly the business of those nominally in charge of educational exchange in the embassy.

In most embassies, furthermore, whether in developed or underdeveloped countries, the Labor Attaché and the Science Attaché, if there are such officers, also engage in activities related to the exchange of persons or ideas. A sample of other federal agencies with important relations to international educational, and cultural affairs includes the Office of Education, the National Institutes of Health, the Children's Bureau, the National Aeronautics and Space Administration, the Coast and Geodetic Survey, the Library of Congress, and the Smithsonian Institution. From time to time, many other departments or agencies will represent the United States in activities with educational, cultural, or scientific significance—for example, commercial and technical exhibits, or participation in the work of special international organizations such as the World Health Organization.

As will be plain, then, the Cultural Affairs Officer is often responsible officially for only a minor segment of the educational and cultural activities carried on by the United States Government in the country to which he is assigned. It should not be assumed without discussion, of course, that the absence of close coordination among various educational and cultural programs is an intrinsically undesirable state of affairs. The Cultural Affairs Officer might do a worse job if the diverse responsibilities of his position were further diversified and extended. Those in charge of special programs—for example, the National Science Foundation program in Japan—may well be able to do a better job when they are themselves specialized in their competence and approach, and have sufficient autonomy to exercise their discretion and initiative. "Coordination" is a vague word, and it is only when it is made more precise, and the mechanisms to be used are stated more definitely, that we can argue usefully about its desirability or undesirability.

Nevertheless, there is at least the scent of a serious problem in the existence in Washington and in embassies of so many separate educational and cultural programs over which no central eye is cast. Duplication of effort, the waste of limited resources, inequities between programs, and confusion about the principles and objectives of American educational and cultural policy are some of the more obvious dangers. Awareness of the need for co-ordination, or, if that is too strong a word, for better communication among programs has existed for some time, both in Washington and in the field. The Secretary of State, and, through him, the Assistant Secretary for Educational and Cultural Affairs, has a general mandate from the President that avoids instructing him to co-ordinate programs, but that authorizes him to lead the way in co-ordination;[8] and the Mutual Educational and Cultural Exchange Act of 1961 (the Fulbright-Hays Act) consolidates and expands international exchange programs, and contains the authority for a more unified approach to the entire field. Efforts at co-ordination, or, as the first Assistant Secretary for Educational and Cultural Affairs, Philip Coombs, prefers to say, efforts "to seek joint solutions to specific problems,"[9] have been made. CU in Washington was reorganized in 1962

[8] As a summary statement this phrasing, I trust, is not inaccurate. It flattens out, however, the subtlety and beauty of the original language: "In order to assure appropriate co-ordination of programs, and taking into account the statutory functions of the departments and other executive agencies concerned, the Secretary of State shall exercise primary responsibility for Government-wide leadership and policy guidance with regard to international educational and cultural affairs." Executive Order 11034, June 25, 1962, sec. 6.

[9] Philip Coombs, *The Fourth Dimension of Foreign Policy—Educational and Cultural Affairs* (Council on Foreign Relations, 1964), p. 46.

on a geographical basis so that it could work in closer harmony with the country desks in the State Department, USIA, and AID. Specific conflicts have at times been eliminated, for example, between the English-teaching programs of USIA and AID in French-speaking Africa, and between the programs of the Peace Corps and AID concerned with sending teachers to East Africa. Regional meetings in the field have brought Cultural Affairs Officers and AID Education Officers together to discuss their problems, and meetings have been held among interested officials in Washington to establish better communication.

OVERLAPPING CIRCLES AND SEPARATE CIRCLES

Despite these efforts, unresolved problems remain. In Washington, although the Assistant Secretary for Educational and Cultural Affairs has a mandate to take an overview of the entire field, the mandate is to a considerable extent an abstraction. The Assistant Secretary lacks the budgetary power to exercise genuine authority, and the Executive Order issued in 1962 represented a compromise among bureaucratic interests that did little to strengthen his hand. A formal division of responsibilities exists—for example, CU is concerned with promoting "mutual understanding," AID with "technical assistance," and USIA with "the American image overseas"—which conforms more closely to the specialized perspectives of different bureaucracies than to the realities of work in the field, where every one of these functions leans on and enhances or diminishes the others.

In the field, there are differences between embassies with respect to these formal divisions of responsibility. In some embassies there is closer communication and articulation than in others. Nevertheless, the remarks that have been made about Washington apply, on the whole, to the field. The Cultural Affairs Officer is usually not in a position, de jure or de facto, to act as a general coordinator of educational and cultural programs. By and large, the degree of coordination that exists is an accident of time, place, and personality. It depends on the desires of the Ambassador, the amount of attention he can give to the job, the mutual compatibility of the various programs involved, the nature of the vested bureaucratic interests concerned, and the character of the individuals who happen to be working in the embassy. If there is a degree of coordination, it is usually produced by committee arrangements and informal personal associations. It rarely rises to the level of systematic and coherent planning.

Indeed, the Cultural Affairs Officer usually knows little about what his government colleagues inside the embassy or next door to it are doing in the field of educational and cultural affairs. The Public Affairs Officer is often better informed, but he is better informed because it is his task to publicize what is being done in the host countries by agencies of the United States Government. His main interest in these programs is not in their organization or objectives but in their utility from the point of view of public relations.

Thus, one set of important issues relating to the conduct of educational and cultural activities arises in consequence of the effort to fit these activities within the general framework of information programs. Another equally important group of issues is posed by the fact that many official American educational and cultural activities fall outside the Cultural Attaché's area of responsibility, and are conducted by a variety of agencies that may or may not maintain close communication with one another. This situation has a double defect. First, educational and cultural policy in a given country is not seen as a single thing; no organizational context exists for doing so. Second, it deprives many educational and cultural programs of the services of the officer in the embassy who may be peculiarly well situated to help them.

An AID-sponsored secondary-school project, for example, may bog down as a result of misunderstanding, indifference, or disagreement on the part of the native teachers and administrators. The Cultural Affairs Officer, if he has been doing his job, is likely to understand some of the cultural and social reasons for these attitudes, and to have friendly and sympathetic relations with many of the host country's leading teachers, intellectuals, and educational administrators. Although he might not succeed in eliminating the difficulties that exist, he will probably be as good a candidate to make the effort as can be found. Yet there is no guarantee that he will be called on to do so. If, by chance, he is, he will confront difficulties which might not have existed in so acute a form if he had been present from the beginning.

3

The Official and Unofficial

WHATEVER DAMAGE THEY MAY CAUSE, the problems that arise from the existence of a multiplicity of separate government programs have at least one comforting feature. Unless an already burdened Cultural Affairs Officer goes out of his way to make them his business, these problems need not bother him. For better or worse, he may know nothing about them, or can choose to ignore them. But this is not the case with regard to another kind of problem which no Cultural Affairs Officer can escape.

Nothing more greatly differentiates international educational and cultural programs from other activities in which the United States Government engages abroad than the degree to which these programs require intimate collaboration between people in public and private life. The Cultural Affairs Officer and his superiors in CU and USIA in Washington must depend, if they are to succeed in what they are trying to do, on the talents, tact, sympathy, and voluntary cooperation of people over whom they have little or no direct authority. Indeed, in general, these people come from sectors of national life—the universities, the stage, the concert hall—where there is an ethic of individual independence and idiosyncrasy, a distrust of administrators and rules, and an inbred suspicion of too close an association with government. While it would be an exaggeration to say that government officials are attempting to reverse an iron law of nature in trying to establish a close and efficient partnership with the educational and cultural communities, it would be an exaggeration that suggests the nature of the problem.

39

ARRANGEMENTS PROTECTING THE PRIVATE SECTOR

Both the complexities and the delicacy of the relationship between the public and private sectors have been recognized in the basic laws governing American international educational and cultural programs. A striking sign of this is the special position given the Board of Foreign Scholarships. Composed mainly of distinguished members of the academic community chosen by presidential appointment, the board is vested with supreme authority for the formation and direction of policy and for the selection of participants in all educational exchange programs under the Fulbright-Hays Act.[1] At the time this legislation was under consideration by Congress, suggestions were made that the authority which the board had enjoyed since the launching of the Fulbright program in 1946 be reduced, and that its responsibility be limited to that of selecting grantees. Not only were these suggestions rejected, but Congress, in the Fulbright-Hays Act, further consolidated the independence and authority of the board, and extended that authority to areas once covered by the Smith-Mundt Act (now superseded), from which the board had previously been excluded. In principle, the Board of Foreign Scholarships enjoys an authority analogous to that possessed by regulative agencies such as the Civil Aeronautics Authority or the Federal Communications Commission. No other lay group, composed of people most of whom are in private life, exercises comparable authority anywhere else in the federal government. It is also noteworthy that the basic initiative for these provisions of the law has come from Congress rather than the Executive branch.

In everyday practice, to be sure, the autonomy and supreme authority of the board is somewhat less clear. The members can devote themselves to the work of the board on only a limited part-time basis, and the board has no independent full-time staff of its own. Whatever the de jure position of the board, these circumstances reduce its de facto powers. Nevertheless, the board has successfully made it plain that its principal raison d'être is to protect the integrity and independence of the educational exchange program. Further, it has registered the fact that the American academic community at large would probably withdraw its support if the board failed to do so. Equally to the point, Congress

[1] *The Mutual Educational and Cultural Exchange Act of 1961,* 75 Stat. 527.

and the Department of State have generally accepted this principle. The fact that the Board of Foreign Scholarships has been as effective as it has, in spite of the considerable practical limitations within which it works, testifies to the essential validity of the principles on which it is based.

An analogous relationship exists abroad between United States embassies and the Bi-National Commissions that have been established in many countries on the basis of agreements between these countries and the United States. These commissions, which supervise exchange programs authorized by the Fulbright-Hays Act, are composed of American citizens resident in the host country and appointed by the Ambassador, and of citizens of the host country appointed by its government. The Ambassador and the Cultural Attaché (or, in some cases, the Educational Exchange Officer, who is usually an Assistant Cultural Affairs Officer) are members. The staff of a commission is composed mainly of citizens of the host country and is headed by an executive secretary, who also may be and often is a citizen of the host country.[2]

There are obvious limits to the authority of these Bi-National Commissions, or Foundations, as they are sometimes called. Since the money for the programs they sponsor comes from the United States Government, they cannot draw up their plans without regard to what the Board of Foreign Scholarships, the Department of State, and, ultimately, the Congress of the United States will approve. However, the potential long-range significance of these commissions with regard to the establishment of reciprocal educational and cultural relations between the United States and other countries may be suggested by the fact that

[2] Parallel in spirit to these Bi-National Commissions, but not to be confused with them, are the important Bi-National Centers operated in many countries with the encouragement and partial support of USIA. Unlike the USIA Information Center, which is closely keyed to the USIA country plan, the Bi-National Center is an indigenous, independent organization, incorporated under the laws of the host country, governed by a Board of Directors composed of local citizens as well as Americans, and staffed by local employees and by Americans who are not in the career service but are recipients of "grants" under which they teach or lead other activities. Instruction in the English language is normally the core of a Bi-National Center's program, but it also offers library facilities and other cultural and social programs. It is supported by tuition fees, membership dues, and donations by private citizens of the host country, as well as by USIA grants when feasible, and it functions with a degree of independence similar to that enjoyed by Bi-National Commissions.

a Bi-National Commission has existed in every country that has made the decision to share the cost with the United States of a Fulbright-Hays exchange program.[3] Such sharing of costs does, of course, present the danger of interference from a new quarter—the host government—with the independence of an exchange program. In Germany, however, where the federal government bears 80 percent of the cost, this danger has not materialized, and, in general, the advantages of reciprocity appear to outweigh the dangers of political influence from other governments. By and large, Bi-National Commissions, which are composed of Americans as well as citizens of the host country, and which number scholars and intellectuals among their most influential members, are as alert to protect the independence of the exchange programs as the Board of Foreign Scholarships in Washington.

Quite apart from these considerations, the Bi-National Commissions usually represent an independent and effective point of view even when the host countries concerned make no financial contribution to the exchange program. The commissions have the status of private foundations, and possess a measure of autonomy with regard to the determination for a given country of Fulbright educational-exchange programs with the United States. Officials in Washington and the field are in general agreement that country programs are not determined by central authority in Washington, but represent the results of negotiation between Washington and the field. And in the field, wherever the foreign members of a Bi-National Commission have been well chosen and there is an effective Executive Secretary, the programs and policies developed represent the results of genuine bi-national consultation, subject to the obvious limitation that such consultation cannot help but be influenced by the fact that the United States Government is normally the principal source of funds. Moreover, the consultation is not simply between governments. It is a four-sided consultation involving representatives of two governments and spokesmen for the educational and cultural communities of two nations.[4]

[3] These countries are Australia, Austria, Denmark, France, the Federal Republic of Germany, Iceland, Norway, Sweden, and the United Kingdom. See the U.S. Department of State Bulletin, Vol. LII (1965), p. 844.

[4] For a more complete discussion of the Board of Foreign Scholarships, the Bi-National Commissions and related matters, see Donald B. Cook and J. Paul Smith, "The Philosophy of the Fulbright Programme," *International Social Science Bulletin*, Vol. VIII, No. 4 (UNESCO, 1957).

In Washington, the programs and policies of CU are also affected by the relationships between CU and the educational and cultural communities. CU receives guidance from the presidentially appointed United States Advisory Commission on International Educational and Cultural Affairs. In its daily activities, it leans heavily on the Conference Board of Associated Research Councils and the Institute of International Education. These private nonprofit organizations, which are related to the learned societies, research councils, and educational groups of the country, act as channels of communication between the educational community and the CU programs.

Other private organizations as well do indispensable work for government educational and cultural programs abroad and exercise, in consequence, a modicum of influence over these programs. To take a few examples, representatives of the African-American Institute offer advisory and testing services in key cities in Africa; the Inter-University Committee on Travel Grants performs basic services for the United States-Soviet Union exchange program, including the conduct of detailed negotiations within the framework of the basic agreement between the two governments; the American Council of Learned Societies, the Social Science Research Council, the National Academy of Sciences, and the American Council on Education (all of which are represented in the Conference Board of Associated Research Councils) are called upon for consultation and cooperation in the development and implementation of educational policy abroad; the American National Theatre and Academy, museums, and similar organizations have played parallel roles in artistic fields. Turning away from CU, a good part of AID's work depends on contractual relations with American universities.[5]

RELATIONSHIP OF THE
PUBLIC AND PRIVATE SECTORS

More important than a detailed description of the intricate network of committees and organizations that tie the public and private sectors together is what lies behind the existence of this network. It exists be-

[5] For further analysis of these relations, see John W. Gardner, *AID and the Universities*, A report to the Administrator of the Agency for International Development (Education and World Affairs, 1964).

cause USIA, CU, AID, and other government agencies engaged in international educational or cultural programs are condemned to failure in these programs unless they can secure the active support of people who do not have to cooperate if they do not wish to, and may even feel a reasoned inclination not to. From this point of view, the problem of establishing effective relationships between the federal government and the educational and cultural communities goes far beyond that of strengthening the existing structure of committees, councils, conference boards, and advisory commissions. These have emerged largely in response to specific problems, and have lingered on to deal with other problems, often very effectively. Their defect, however, is that they are not substitutes for more fundamental arrangements that do not now exist, and that are necessary to promote a sense of mutual trust and joint responsibility between the worlds of education, scholarship, the arts and sciences on one hand and the world of Congress, officialdom, and foreign affairs on the other.

The absence of adequate mutual understanding between these two worlds is indicated by a number of currently disturbing problems. There has been increasing difficulty for some years, for example, in the recruitment of first-rate senior scholars to take part in the Fulbright program. Among the circumstances responsible for this state of affairs is the fact that funds have never been made available to meet the cost of travel of a scholar's dependents. Although increasingly attractive opportunities for study, teaching, and travel have been made available to outstanding scholars by universities, private foundations, and a variety of government agencies, scholars who wish to participate in the Fulbright exchange program must continue to pay for the privilege. Yet, although the Fulbright-Hays Act specifically authorizes grants in support of dependents' travel, and although the Department of State has regularly requested that the funds be appropriated, the House Appropriations Committee has annually stricken such requests from the budget. In the eyes of those responsible for the practical conduct of the exchange program, this constitutes a formidable handicap to recruitment.

The difficulties caused by this state of affairs have also been aggravated in the past by the paucity of short-term grants, which are often the only grants that busy scholars of the first rank are in a position to accept. More recently, there has been a greater willingness to offer awards for short periods, in some instances as short as two weeks. However, it still remains the case that better techniques for using the services of top-ranking scholars for short periods are needed. Such scholars might well be used not only to give lectures, but to study the needs and desires of a host country with regard to their discipline, and to make appropriate suggestions to those in charge of planning exchange programs. In this way, the active interest of leaders of American scholarship in exchange programs might be more effectively encouraged.

Indeed, in the precarious partnership between the government and the independent scholarly community, it is by no means Congress or government officials alone that exhibit a lack of close sympathy with the attitudes and needs of people on the other side. The acceptance of a grant that takes a scholar away from the campus is often frowned on by university administrators, and is sometimes regarded not as the performance of academic duties but as an escape from these duties. Teaching abroad is not sufficiently accepted as a normal part of an academic career, and the man who accepts such assignments may find not only that they are not taken into account when matters of tenure and promotion are raised, but that he may suffer in comparison with those who have stayed at home. This is particularly discouraging to younger scholars, who might be eager to participate in government programs.

Given the pressures on American colleges and universities to meet the enormous demands being made on them at home, it is intelligible that such attitudes exist. There are, obviously, limits to the resources, particularly in competent teachers and scholars, which colleges and universities can divert to international activities. Precisely because resources are scarce, however, the case for creating a framework for continuing consultation and planning is strong. Existing shortages of resources, existing wastage of effort, and existing misunderstandings between the government and the scholarly community are all fixed into place by the absence of a system that might permit the government and the universities to weigh priorities, and to address themselves jointly to the problem of bringing needs and resources into some relationship to one another. The pattern of cooperation with regard to international educational affairs that now exists between the government and the scholarly community is often effective with respect to specific problems. Still, it resembles less an alliance to attack a common set of problems than a set of ad hoc, and often uneasy, arrangements between two sides, neither of which is convinced that the other understands its problems.

This is illustrated by other difficulties that have arisen in recruiting senior scholars for the exchange program. In recent years, there has been a growing concern on the part of CU to use Fulbright grants to aid the development of the poorer nations. Nor is this a radical departure from hitherto accepted principles. As the Smith-Mundt Act attests, technical assistance has from an early stage been regarded as one of the essential purposes of educational exchange. However, the State Department has experienced difficulties in finding appropriate people to do the jobs it wants. Some of the reasons for this failure to fit needs and resources together appear to lie in present procedures for developing exchange programs, and in misunderstandings about where the practical responsibility lies for the formulation and implementation of these programs.

In the discussions that I have had with them, leaders of the scholarly organizations that are represented on the Committee on International Exchange of Persons of the Conference Board of Associated Research Councils have stated that they have the feeling, more often than not, that their organizations are confronted with plans which they have had no part in formulating. Representatives of the State Department, in contrast, have reminded me that neither CU nor the Board of Foreign Scholarships has ever placed any constraints on the Conference Board with regard to its bringing scholars more substantially into the planning process; from the point of view of these officials, the failure of scholarly organizations to take active responsibility for the criticism or development of country plans is the fault of these organizations. The allocation of blame for this state of affairs, however, is not the point. Whether one side, the other side, or neither side is to blame, the situation is clearly marked by "sides," and by inadequate two-way communication.

As presently constituted, the exchange plan for an individual country is largely the product of consultation among the Bi-National Commission for the country, the Cultural Affairs Officer on the spot, the Ambassador, and CU in Washington. Toward the end of this process, the staff of the Conference Board (or, when appropriate, the Institute of International Education) is asked to comment, although it must do so within the severe limitations of time and program; and, after the plan is more or less set, the problem of finding the people to fulfill it is turned over to the Conference Board or to other agencies. To be sure, modifications of the original country plan take place. On one side, the Bi-National Commission normally consults the universities in its country to determine what faculty members can be spared to accept awards, and what American grantees the universities wish to invite or are prepared to accept. On the other side, the Conference Board, apart from the country plan, often nominates people from among those who have independently applied for exchange grants. Thus, a country plan is subject to change as it turns out to be impossible to fill certain requests, or to be possible to undertake worthwhile programs that were not originally requested. It is also plain that the plan that a Bi-National Commission presents in any given year reflects the accumulated experiences from the past, and, in particular, the comments of the Conference Board on previous plans. All this, however, is far from a process of genuine consultative planning, involving the careful survey of long-range needs or the circumspect selection of key targets. Although give-and-take occurs, the definitive characteristic of the present relationship between the government and the academic community is that the latter serves primarily as a jobber for the former.

At no point in the process are appropriate American scholars—leaders in the disciplines directly concerned, spokesmen for professional societies, or area specialists—asked to participate, in a systematic and regularized way, in the making of specific country plans. At best, they serve on screening committees, which have a subordinate function. Recognition of this problem exists in CU, and some interesting experiments have begun in an effort to deal with it. If they are successful, it may be hoped that they will be extended to correct what is now a fundamental defect in the basic scheme of cooperation between government and the learned community. Despite the authority enjoyed de jure by the Board of Foreign Scholarships, the American academic community is not yet a full partner in the planning process, contributing its expertise to the examination of the needs of individual countries and disciplines. At least with respect to the large category of grants for American scholars to teach abroad, if not with respect to research and study grants, the academic community remains an instrument for carrying out other people's plans. Analogously, when requests are made to individuals to take part in these programs, they come from the government or one of its liaison agencies; they do not come directly through educational or scholarly channels—through university administrations or the scholar's professional society.

The difficulties encountered by government agencies in finding the qualified people they are looking for appear to be a consequence in some measure of this state of affairs. Plans are made without asking the people who are going to carry them out whether they are realistic or whether better plans might not be made. The search for the right people takes place only partly through the established channels that lend authority to an effort to recruit an individual; and it is often difficult to describe the work to be done abroad in convincing scholarly and educational terms, terms that reflect either an expert appraisal of overseas needs or an understanding of the specific way in which the visiting scholar can use his specialized talents in the position to which he will be assigned. In such circumstances, it is not likely that a mechanistic approach to the improvement of existing recruitment and screening procedures will remove the principal source of the trouble. Undoubtedly, these procedures can be improved; procedures always can be. But the issue is not, in the end, a procedural one; it has to do with the atmosphere and the institutional framework in which planning for educational and cultural exchange takes place.

Analogous difficulties have arisen in the relationship between AID and the universities. Writing about this relationship, John Gardner observes:

> The nature of the complaints is familiar enough. The Universities say that AID lags far behind other agencies, such as the National Science Foundation and the Office of Naval Research (to name only two), in its understanding of the universities. They say that AID doesn't grasp the nature and purposes of universities, doesn't know how to use them wisely, doesn't allow them to make the distinctive contribution that only they can make. If AID really understood these things, say the universities, the Agency would take a more generous view of the research component in contracts; would not devise and administer contracts so rigid and detailed as to frustrate the purposes they are designed to further; would take a more generous view of the kind of contract provisions that would strengthen the university itself, and would not insist on measuring contract performance by externals and expecting precise evidence of short-term accomplishment.
>
> AID responds that the universities make no attempt to understand its problems—its constant need to justify its actions to Congress, its inescapable responsibility for program decisions, its accountability

to the taxpayers. It points out that universities have often acted irresponsibly—sending third-rate personnel overseas, neglecting the needs of the host country while they concentrate on what *they* want to do, engaging in aggressive tactics to get contracts, taking on tasks they are not equipped to do well, failing to put the full weight and resources of the university behind a contract and so on. Some AID officials add that no United States university ever willingly terminated a contract program, no matter how valid the reasons for doing so.

Though some of these complaints are exaggerated, they are not manufactured out of thin air. Both sides can produce *some* evidence to support their assertions.[6]

Such mutual complaints are perhaps natural up to a point. When they rigidify into standard and standing grievances, they are symptoms of a fundamental issue, which existing arrangements for cooperation between government and the intellectual, educational, and artistic worlds have not resolved. The fundamental and ineluctable fact on which all government programs in international cultural affairs rise or fall is that the government is dealing in something which it does not produce, and which, given the habits and principles of free government, it has neither the power nor the right to regulate and control. An educational and cultural program exports what is by nature unofficial, and what has not normally been created—at any rate, if it is of high quality—to suit the special needs of a government program.

An effective educational and cultural program therefore requires something more than ad hoc consultative arrangements that bring government officials and representatives of the arts, sciences, and education together. It requires a framework for cooperation that permits a continuing joint survey and overview of common problems, and encourages a joint attack on them. This is necessary not only to ensure that American educational and cultural programs abroad have been adequately illuminated by the special knowledge and perspectives of educators and scholars. It is necessary if universities, scholarly organizations, and individual scholars are to feel a continuing proprietary interest in the outcome of such programs. Such an interest, not the interest of a party to a contract or of a grantee in his sabbatical year but the interest of an initiator and trustee, is a sine qua non for strengthening these programs to any substantial extent.

[6] Gardner, *op. cit.*

Indeed, this chapter would be incomplete if it left the impression that current difficulties are chiefly due to the failings of government officials. If there is inadequate communication between government and the academic community, this is due in part to the fact that, so far as international educational and cultural affairs are concerned, the phrase "the academic community" is as much a fiction-writer's term as a sober descriptive reporter's. In this field, members of the academic world have not yet come together in a practical and continuing way to examine their common interests and responsibilities, and to establish among themselves a recognized framework for discussing principles, exchanging information, and sharing resources.

On paper, the Conference Board's Committee on International Exchange of Persons may be thought to serve that function in part. But that committee itself is composed of people chosen by four research councils—the American Council on Education, the American Council of Learned Societies, the National Research Council of the National Academy of Sciences, and the Social Science Research Council. These councils are themselves loose federations of scholarly organizations, and the extent to which the scholarly community is actively consulted or engaged or "scholarly opinion" communicated through these channels is probably not very great. Plainly, the scholarly community must give serious thought on its own to the way in which it organizes itself.

While there is a measure of faith and hope, however, and perhaps of charity, in speaking of an "academic community" in relation to international educational and cultural affairs, there is also some descriptive truth in such statements. The major scholarly organizations that are accepted as legitimate spokesmen for scholarly and educational interests are easily identified, and they give some substance to the belief that an academic community exists. At important moments in the development of the United States Government's educational and cultural policies abroad—for example, at the time that the Fulbright-Hays Act was under consideration—the accredited representatives of these organizations have stated their views with force and have acted in a concerted manner. Over the years, too, a large number of ad hoc committees and organizations have arisen to deal with issues requiring the collaboration of government and private educational institutions. In the process, new habits, new administrative experience, and new foci of interest have emerged that provide the basis for a more ambitious and systematic attack on common problems.

The emergence of the new private foundation, Education and World Affairs, is a symbol of these developments and of the recognition that they are only a prologue to what can be done. Moreover, the international involvement of the educational institutions of the United States has grown enormously, as is indicated by the adoption of programs for a junior year abroad, the increasingly sophisticated arrangements being made for foreign students, the widespread introduction of area-studies, and the participation in extensive programs of educational and technical assistance overseas. What is required is the organization and amplification of an interest that exists, not the creation of such an interest.

As further steps are contemplated, it is important to recognize that while government may act as a stimulant and catalyst, major responsibility for action rests with scholars and educational institutions. A renewed interest on the part of many university people in American foreign policy has recently been brought forcefully to public attention. It is to be hoped that some of this renewed interest and sense of common scholarly responsibility will also flow into that area of American foreign relations to which teachers and scholars can contribute most directly.

4

The Controlling Audiences

IMPORTANT AS THE QUESTIONS ARE that have just been discussed, apparatus would be confused with policy if our examination of the forces that play on the United States educational and cultural programs ended at this point. For beyond the relations of the Cultural Affairs Officer with CU and USIA, beyond the relations of federal programs with one another, beyond even the intricate problems posed by the interdependence of the public and private sectors, the United States Government's educational and cultural programs abroad are influenced by the attitudes and expectations of audiences that are not directly responsible for the implementation of educational and cultural policy. And it is the reactions of these audiences that provide ı large part, the first practical measure of the success of these programs.

The two principal audiences are the intellectuals and the politicians. The intellectuals are a social category the Duke of Wellington once labeled with less than complete affection, "the scribbling set"; the politicians, for our purposes, may be taken to be the members of the United States Congress. In the largest terms, the practical, everyday task of those responsible for American educational and cultural activities abroad is to develop programs that will appeal successfully to both groups. As anyone might guess, this is not an easy job.

COMMUNICATION BETWEEN AMERICAN
INTELLECTUALS AND INTELLECTUALS ABROAD

Plainly enough, the principal audience abroad for United States educational and cultural programs is composed of "the intellectuals" —university students, teachers, writers, scholars, cultural leaders, and members of the learned professions.[1] Even when educational or cultural programs have other audiences in mind, these groups play a pivotal role. AID's educational projects may in many places aim more specifically at primary and secondary school students, but without the understanding and cooperation of local teachers, school administrators, and officials of education ministries they are not likely to succeed. Some of CU's cultural presentations—for example, a jazz band or a touring movie star—may aim at a mass audience, but, similarly, their reception depends to a considerable extent on the amount and kind of attention they receive from editors, critics, and broadcasters. Of all United States agencies conducting large educational programs abroad, probably only the Peace Corps can achieve its purposes without major reliance on the good will of foreign intellectuals; and even its programs can be compromised by these groups if they wish to do so.

The attitudes of intellectual groups abroad are therefore extremely relevant to an understanding of the nature of the task with which those responsible for the conduct of American educational and cultural programs are confronted. It is tempting, and common, to lump these attitudes together under the general heading of "anti-Americanism." But this is almost certainly misleading. The attitudes to which this label is applied are not infrequently accompanied by great courtesy and friendship toward individual Americans, by avid interest in American intellectual, literary, and artistic achievements, and even by basic sympathy with the long-range objectives of United States foreign policy. "Anti-Americanism," so-called, is in fact a complex and elusive phenomenon composed of many separate strands, a good number of which have little to do intrinsically with American culture as such. Instead of concentrating on anti-Americanism, which begs many questions, it is preferable to try to unravel these strands and to see what they imply with regard to the problem of communication between articulate representatives of American and foreign cultures.

Obviously, there are grave dangers of oversimplification in any attempt to characterize the intellectuals of the United States or of other countries in a few broad strokes. The ethnic, social, and political differences between the intellectuals of different countries are frequently very

---

[1] See the footnote, p. 75 below, for a fuller account of the meaning of the phrase, "the intellectuals," as it is used here.

great, and, within individual countries, intellectual groups are commonly divided into subgroups and factions that are in sharp disagreement with one another. So far as the remarks that are about to be made are concerned, it should be borne in mind that they describe, on the whole, the attitudes of the most vocal and visible members of intellectual groups, and that they apply with least force to the English-speaking and Scandinavian countries, and probably with greatest force to the intellectuals of the emerging countries. It should also be stressed that we are discussing differences between American intellectuals and intellectuals elsewhere that are differences in degree, matters of more or less, and not absolute, categorical contrasts. There are American intellectuals whose general stance and tone are indistinguishable from those of intellectuals elsewhere. There are foreign intellectuals who differ in no significant respect from what is here described as the modal pattern for the United States. Within the framework of such reservations, however, a number of generalizations may be hazarded.

To begin with, the basic intellectual perspective of the dominant groups in the intellectual circles of most foreign countries tends to be different from that which prevails among most leading representatives of American scholarship and intellectual life. Setting aside specialists in the physical sciences, the education and mental formation of most foreign intellectuals is literary in character, and their approach to social issues is marked by a high degree of reliance on broad and abstract theories and ideals. In contrast, American scholars, particularly those in the social sciences, tend to be more empirical, more concerned with refined problems of methodology, and more anti-ideological. Where foreign intellectuals enjoy using comprehensive intellectual schemes, often carrying heavy philosophical and metaphysical overtones, to explain and interpret specific trends, American scholars and social observers tend to be skeptical, perhaps overly skeptical, of broad generalizations and value-judgments.

This difference in basic intellectual outlook leads to other differences. They are differences that are sometimes more apparent than real, but they are important nonetheless, because they are felt to be real. Thus, to a considerable extent, intellectuals abroad are likely to be leftist in their political sentiments. In contrast, American scholars and intellectuals, although, in fact, they may be anything but conservative, are nevertheless frequently perceived by their foreign colleagues as adherents of the status quo. The reason has less to do with their explicit political sentiments than with their intellectual style. By and large, they tend to be "problem-oriented." They generally shun, that is to say, sweeping verdicts on the state of society, and prefer, by training and inclination, to break down large issues into their smaller parts, formulating these as limited problems which manageable programs of inquiry or reform may reasonably be expected to solve. Accordingly, to others with different traditions, American scholars are likely to seem at best mildly reformist or meliorist. Their concern to deal with limited problems one by one suggests that they are merely tinkering with a social system with whose fundamental aspects they are in sympathy.

Moreover, this impression, which foreign intellectuals have of American intellectual culture, is complemented and complicated by another impression which they are also likely to have. Leftist though they may be in their political sentiments, many foreign intellectuals also tend to be aristocratic in their educational, esthetic, and cultural ideals. Although American intellectuals may often share the foreigner's disdain for "leveling-downwards" and "mass culture," they are less often as stringent and uncompromising in their declarations of principle. They are likely to be more tolerant of the theory and practice of American mass education. They are less prone to see inherent conflicts between "democracy" and "excellence," or "industrial society" and "individual freedom." While they may recognize a conflict between "the sciences" and "the humanities," they do not so often draw the absolute line between these two spheres that intellectuals in other parts of the world do. In sum, although an antagonism between "the two cultures" exists in the United States, it is probably less pronounced in this country than in any other. In consequence, if American intellectuals strike others as too conservative from one point of view, they also often seem too modernist, too supinely afloat on the wave of the future, from another point of view.[2]

---

[2] Although we are not discussing established facts about American intellectuals, but only the views which intellectuals elsewhere tend to hold of them, some apparently important exceptions to these generalizations may nevertheless come to mind. Men like Robert Oppenheimer or Linus Pauling are obviously not perceived either as conservatives or as apologists for technocracy by intellectuals abroad. Again, the activities of many American professors with regard to civil rights or Vietnam would seem to fall into the pattern of political activity characteristic of the most

The issue is practical, indeed economic and political, as well as moral and theoretical. The introduction of new intellectual materials that require new intellectual skills if they are to be mastered, particularly the introduction of methods of social inquiry marked by indifference to traditional ideological positions, has encountered resistance on many occasions and in many places in the United States. This resistance is likely to be all the greater when, in a given country, such materials and methods appear to be an import from abroad. A revision of secondary-school curricula, the return of students trained in the United States in American methods of empirical social inquiry, the introduction by visiting American scholars of the American style in sociology and political science, can all imply or seem to imply the upsetting of established learning in a host country. Without intending to do so, American programs of educational and cultural exchange can thus threaten the established system of status and prestige in academic and intellectual circles abroad.

To this must be added other sources of potential misunderstanding. The labels that American and foreign intellectuals use to discuss social systems are different. Discussions by most foreign intellectuals still turn on words like "socialism" and "capitalism," the former being almost invariably a eulogistic term, the latter almost invariably pejorative. It is difficult for foreign intellectuals to join issue with intellectuals like those from the United States, who seem so often to be indifferent to

visible and vocal intellectual circles abroad. And there are, of course, well-known intellectual journals of opinion in the United States, usually literary in their focus, whose tone of alienation from contemporary American culture resembles the tone of similar journals abroad.

Nevertheless, while these examples indicate that the contrast must be carefully shaded, they also underscore its basic truth. Dr. Pauling, for example, has been a radical critic of United States military policy, and Dr. Oppenheimer has gained fame not only as physicist but as a social philosopher concerned about the relation of science to humanistic civilization. Yet neither can be identified either as the spokesman or the critic of a general political position that can be given ideological formulation. Again, there is no evidence that the great majority of professors who have taken part in Vietnam demonstrations are critics of the American political or social system in general, or even that they are opposed to the major aspects of United States foreign policy such as NATO or foreign aid. Turning to such literary journals of opinion as, for example, *The New York Review of Books*, we find in them not only a high content of ideology, but also a high content of anti-ideology. To foreign intellectuals, at any rate, all this is likely to suggest that American intellectuals are strangely indifferent, or perhaps even hostile, to questions of first principles.

the distinction intended by these words, and who tend to suggest, indeed, that the words are misleading.

There are allied difficulties in connection with attitudes toward religion. In many other countries, the intellectuals, particularly the younger ones, are predominantly not religious or are militantly anti-religious. At the very least, they are not usually Protestant Christians, and are therefore likely to be puzzled or put off by the special religious rhetoric that characterizes many American political statements. Even if American scholars and intellectuals do not echo this rhetoric, they may still puzzle their foreign counterparts. For there is little in the experience of the latter to prepare them to understand attitudes toward religion —ranging from ingenious reconstructions of traditional religious thought through cheerful tolerance of all religion to mild indifference to the religious question—which are likely to characterize intellectuals who have grown up in a society where religious pluralism is well established.

Such differences in outlook are sharpened by differences in the history and in the social position and function of intellectual groups in the United States and other countries. Students, scholars, writers, and artists abroad tend to be discriminable and visible groups in their society. Often, they have relatively little active contact with other social groups. Indeed, they often perceive themselves, and are perceived, as a separate social *class*, with a distinct outlook and a special social mission. They are the vanguard of the forces of enlightenment, the spokesmen for modernization or freedom or the emerging national culture, the keepers of the national conscience. American intellectuals, in comparison, have less ambitious conceptions of their role, and less consciousness of themselves as a class, just as American businessmen, workers, and government functionaries also tend to have less class-consciousness.

This difference between American intellectuals and intellectuals abroad runs parallel to another. By and large, foreign intellectuals think of themselves as performing their special functions precisely when they keep their distance from the centers of power governing their society. They are prepared to identify themselves with the powers that be only when, in turn, they can identify these powers that be with themselves—only when they believe, that is to say, that government, the economy, and the social structure are being systematically rebuilt in accordance with the principles of intellectuals. From such a point of view, it is one thing to take and use power for "revolutionary" purposes; it is quite another thing to serve those who have power and who use it merely to keep things going or to patch things up. Accordingly, for many foreign intellectuals, to advise government, to counsel industry, to bring technical expertise to bear on specific social problems, seems to be equivalent to the renunciation of one's status as an intellectual. American scholars, in contrast, are less inclined to regard a close identification with power as inherently contaminating. They find it easier to think of practical service to government, industry, or the community in neutral, nonpolitical terms.

It is worth saying again that these are only differences in degree. There are a number of American scholars and intellectuals who regard any form of close association with government or industry as an abandonment of their intellectual independence. And there are many scholars and intellectuals, not only in Western Europe, but in Asia, Africa, and Latin America, who have undertaken practical tasks of leadership and counseling, and have moved back and forth between the universities, the professions, and government service. But to some extent this reflects the tempo of development and the shortage of manpower in the emerging countries; and to some extent it reflects the congruence of the official revolutionary ideologies of these countries with the principles of the scholars and intellectuals concerned. Broadly speaking, even though the difference between American and foreign intellectuals may be a matter of degree, it remains a significant difference. Fewer American scholars and students think of themselves as generalized intellectuals; they think of their social role simply as that of men possessing special knowledge, like doctors or engineers. More foreign scholars and students are self-consciously intellectuals, and think of their social role as that of secular priests—general guides, critics, and judges of their society.

Behind these different attitudes toward identification with power, there are often, of course, objective differences in the social situation and political realities of different countries. In many countries in Latin America, for example, the people who hold power in government or the economy are deeply hostile both to intellectuals and to social reform. It is not a mistake or a dogmatic ideological illusion for an intellectual in such circumstances to view an alliance with power as defection from principle. But behind such attitudes toward identification with power, there are also certain pervasive attitudes toward power itself. The notion that political practice is inescapably a moral compromise goes back to Plato, pervades Western philosophy and Western common sense, and has become part of the heritage of intellectuals in most countries in the world. In the West, it is reinforced by traditional suspicions of worldly pomp and power inherited from Prophetic and Christian teachings. In many other civilizations, it is reinforced by religious and philosophical ideas that condemn the material world as the scene of illusion and temptation. And just as in the West, people may hold such views who proclaim themselves materialists.

In any case, whatever their sources, such views are widespread, and they have considerable influence in many parts of the world on intellectual attitudes toward power, and, indeed, toward the very nature of politics, government, and social authority. Given such inherited attitudes toward power and identification with it, it should not be surprising that intellectual groups abroad—or, at any rate, some of the most articulate and influential elements among them—should be negatively predisposed toward American society and American policy. To be critical of power almost automatically entails that one be critical of the country that, above all others, possesses and epitomizes worldly success, wealth, and influence. Needless to say, American deeds and pronouncements also have much to do with the attitudes toward the United States of intellectuals abroad. But it is naive to imagine, so long as the United States occupies the position in the world that it does, and so long as the intellectuals of most other societies retain their traditional cast of mind with regard to their social mission and their relation to power, that American policy will not have to contend with a basic undertow of suspicion against it on the part of intellectuals in other countries.

Finally, major historical trends affect and complicate the relationship of American culture to other cultures. In the emerging societies, intellectuals are usually committed to the modernization of their society, and resent any implication that they are less "progressive" in their thinking than their fellow intellectuals in the West. In practical terms, this means that they are eager to show themselves to be, in significant respects, Westernized. At the same time, they cannot help but associate Western culture with a memory of injustice and of the subordination of their own native culture. In consequence, they often have equivocal feelings toward Western culture, including its American version. This is one reason for the appeal of Marxism, a philosophy which, at one and the same time, offers both a convenient synthesis of Western tradition and a radical critique of that tradition. Marxism allows the intellectual of non-Western societies to feel that he is taking advantage of Western thought without being taken in by it. In contrast, any United States program of educational or cultural exchange with a developing country, much as it may be to the interest of both sides, almost inevitably raises the spectre of "cultural imperialism."

In the emerging nations, Americans may hear their country accused of playing a devious and self-interested game. In the more developed nations, they may hear United States policy condemned for its innocence and optimism. Nevertheless, while the difficulties that appear in relations with the intellectuals of the developed countries are not quite the same as those that affect relations with the underdeveloped countries, they are in certain respects analogous. Feelings of national pride, American and foreign, play a role in the process of cultural communication between the United States and other economically advanced societies, and the events of the last quarter-century have exacerbated these feelings. In Japan, it cannot help but be difficult for intellectuals to separate their response to American culture from their memory of defeat, occupation, and tutelage by the Americans. In Western Europe, the American presence is a standing reminder of a war in which everybody in the West but the Americans suffered a major loss of status. In the circumstances, an emphasis on the unfitness of the United States for leadership—on the incongruence between America's economic and military power and its cultural immaturity—is perhaps to be expected.

Moreover, underneath these feelings there is a deeper one, akin to the feelings of those in the emerging countries who fear "cultural imperialism." It is anger at the destruction of hereditary standards and amenities by the advance of technology and the mass market. The juke box, the snack bar, the traffic jam, the supermarket, and the patterns of aspiration and emulation they symbolize, have become universal phenomena in developed nations. They suggest the coming of a homogenized international civilization which people who like their own native idiosyncrasies are bound to resent and resist. When they do so, there is a natural tendency for them to resent and resist American culture. For these phenomena have been carried to their most extreme form in the United States, and are associated with a process known around the world as "Americanization."

The association is in fact largely adventitious. The United States is undoubtedly the most conspicuous example of a country that has plunged heavily into the process variously known as "modernization" or "industrialization." But other countries have now also plunged heavily into this process, and their changing style of life reflects the changed opportunities and aspirations of their own populations rather than American pressure or propaganda. As has often been observed, there are no laws forcing people elsewhere to queue up to see Hollywood movies, to leave domestic service for work in factories, to import American slang into their language, or to strive to obtain the products of mass-production, American style. They seem to have made such choices of their own free will. Nevertheless, even though the United States may simply be a convenient scapegoat on which these revolutionary changes can be blamed, the fact remains that there are special overtones in the relationship of foreign intellectuals to American culture. For American culture, or what is thought to be American culture, is a lively and painful domestic issue in their own societies—not a piece of exotica, or another country's way of life, but a living example and option for their own country in which they must acquiesce or against which they must struggle.

CULTURAL EXCHANGE AS A CULTURAL PROBLEM

It may seem that insurmountable obstacles lie in the path of good educational and cultural relations between the United States and other countries. But this view is tenable only if it is assumed that the basic objective of educational and cultural exchange is to help the United States win an international popularity contest or to persuade others of the soundness of this year's Multi-Lateral Force or next year's Grand Design. In terms of such assumptions, the issues that have been mentioned constitute formidable roadblocks. Indeed, policies based on such assumptions, far from being able to overcome these problems, are likely to aggravate them considerably. For they tend to treat educational and cultural affairs simply as the "soft-sell" department of the American diplomatic and propaganda effort. If the United States were not so powerful as it is, such an approach, just possibly, would have a greater chance of success. Given the facts that exist, this approach is probably unrealistic even from a purely propagandistic point of view.

It is not necessary, however, to approach the problems mentioned from this point of view. Another and more correct inference that can be drawn from this recital of the difficulties affecting cultural communication between the United States and other countries is that cultural relations between nations are a cultural problem, to be dealt with in its own terms. Political conflicts that affect cultural relations cannot be overcome by the political manipulation of cultural activities. When misunderstandings or genuinely adverse interests and outlooks lead to cultural conflicts, these can be mitigated only by an autonomous dialogue among the students, scholars, and intellectuals concerned, speaking not as representatives of the power interests of their nations but as people with a common interest in things of the mind.

The problems that have been mentioned are not barriers to effective cultural communication between the United States and other countries unless they are treated as such. The fact is that they can also be treated as problems that constitute potential ties between the United States and these countries. The overhanging problem of using technological progress to enhance rather than to destroy humane values and the esthetic quality of life is a prime example. With regard to this problem, the United States is in no position to give instruction to others; neither are other nations in a position to point the finger of scorn at the United States. It is a problem for all industrial civilizations and for all societies moving toward industrialization, and it invites not the exchange of boasts, complaints, or invidious comparisons, but joint concern and inquiry.

A sense of community can be developed not only by an announcement of common values but by a sense of common problems that are shared. The exchange of ideas and information as part of a common effort to face such problems can lead to the discovery of common values and aspirations where they had not been suspected before. Nor does this apply only to encompassing social and moral problems such as the one that has been mentioned. It applies as well to the more limited professional problems of scholars, writers, and artists. Despite the difficulties of communication between the intellectuals of different nations, the experience of those who have participated in exchange programs makes it plain that the establishment of effective communication is a plausible and realistic objective. It also indicates that communication is normally most effective when the common business of students, scholars, and intellectuals is kept at the center of attention, and other matters are kept at the fringe.

THE CONGRESSIONAL AUDIENCE

These remarks take us to the second important audience that exercises influence on the character and success of the United States Government's educational and cultural activities abroad. In all the decisions regarding these activities that are made in Washington or the field, attention to the past or prospective reactions of Congress is inevitably a significant ingredient. The international educational and cultural programs of the United States must gain acceptance not only from intellectuals abroad but from congressmen and senators at home. At least sometimes, it is an open question to which of these audiences these programs are primarily addressed. In any event, Cultural and Public Affairs Officers and AID Education Officers almost invariably report the difficulties of mediating between the attitudes and demands of these two groups.

Yet it is not possible to attribute to senators and congressmen any single set of attitudes with regard to the nature and function of educational and cultural activities abroad. On the one hand, it is unmistakable that some congressmen are indifferent to these programs, that others are doubtful they are worth their cost, and that still others, though favorably disposed, fail to grasp the nature of some of the peculiar problems these programs present. On the other hand, Congress, it is of considerable moment to note, has at every crucial juncture been consistent and clear with regard to a central issue. In the basic legislation authorizing the government to undertake educational and cultural exchange programs, the principle that these programs should enjoy independence from politics and propaganda has been regularly reaffirmed.

The fact appears to be that the opinions that exist in Congress with regard to educational and cultural affairs are varied and diverse, and cover a wide spectrum. It is probably the spectrum of opinion that exists in American society at large. In dealing with the relation of the congressional audience to American educational and cultural activities abroad, the problem confronting the United States, therefore, is not so much a matter of the special opinions of congressmen—their opinions do not appear to be special—as it is a matter of their special political situation, their constitutional functions, and their established modes of procedure. Most politicians are not scribblers; they have their own problems and duties, and their own point of view. They need not be either indifferent or hostile to international educational and cultural exchange. But the local responsibilities of congressmen, their budgetary procedures, and the particular committee organization of the Senate and the House, have led to certain recurrent issues.

The practice of year-by-year budgeting, for example, has encouraged the application of short-range criteria of success to educational and cultural programs, and the practice of considering foreign aid in a single omnibus bill has encouraged the subordination of such programs to more immediate crises and goals of foreign policy. Senator Fulbright, the Chairman of the Senate Foreign Relations Committee, has maintained that the practice of combining all forms of foreign aid in a single package is detrimental to programs of economic assistance, causing them to be unduly subject to passing waves of emotion, and setting them in the wrong frame of reference for evaluating them.[3] Even if one rejects this thesis with respect to economic aid, it appears to be a sound one with respect to educational and cultural programs, whose objectives are even more long-range than those of economic assistance programs, and whose accomplishments, however significant they may be, are not susceptible to easy measurement.

Moreover, the constitutional position of congressmen and senators vis-à-vis the activities of Executive agencies puts them in a special relationship to educational and cultural programs. They are trustees, not operators. What is likely to come to their attention are accidents, mistakes, crises, and scandals. A Peace Corps girl's trek across the Sahara on holiday, a visiting scholar's past Communist affiliation, a returning Fulbright grantee's acid remarks about Vietnam, can therefore put entire programs of quiet and effective international cooperation on the

---

[3] J. W. Fulbright, "Foreign Aid? Yes, But With a New Approach," *New York Times Magazine*, March 21, 1965.

defensive. It is also reasonable that congressmen and senators, who are guardians of the nation's purse strings, should be anxious to look for results when they authorize the expenditure of taxpayers' money. Some have a tendency, therefore, to look at educational and cultural programs primarily as instruments in the building of an American national "image," and to measure their effectiveness in terms of such things as friendly coverage in the foreign press or favorable votes in the United Nations. That these are relevant tests, given enough time, cannot be denied; that they are central purposes of educational and cultural exchange is less evident. Indeed, there occasionally appears to be greater interest in projecting an image of the United States abroad which Congress and the American people will approve than in projecting an image that will win the approval of people elsewhere. As veteran public relations people report in their candid moments, the subject of a public relations campaign is often less interested in persuading others than in having his own ego massaged.

Congress must also regularly deal with threats and crises in all parts of the world that demand an immediate expenditure of funds. International educational and cultural programs are often the first to suffer. In this respect, these programs labor under a peculiar disadvantage. Crises do not necessarily bring them support; they may drive it away.

Nevertheless, this study describes only tendencies and not iron laws. Moreover, they are tendencies that are less conspicuous now than they were a decade ago. Indeed, the most significant fact in the history of congressional attitudes toward international educational and cultural activities is not the existence of such tendencies. They are, after all, only to be expected. The most significant fact is the growth over the years of congressional understanding and respect for educational and cultural programs, and their gradual establishment in the congressional mind as an integral part of the total American effort abroad.

In the end, the problems that continue to exist can be put down only at their periphery to the vagaries of individual congressmen. They arise not so much because congressmen and senators as a group are opposed to educational and cultural programs, but because the House and the Senate have certain established habits and procedures for dealing with such programs. Educational and cultural exchange is normally presented to Congress for consideration in the context of diplomatic, economic, or propaganda policy. No regular context exists for presenting these activities in their own terms, as independent components of the American people's relations with the rest of the world. Nor has the American academic community—to return to a central issue—made itself heard as an organized group expressing a systematic and coherent interest in international educational and cultural activity. If congressmen and senators have their local responsibilities and sectional preoccupations, many members of the academic world as well are preoccupied by loyalties to their specific disciplines, and their sense of allegiance to their profession as a whole is fitful.

But a whole array of issues, administrative, political, psychological, and intellectual, are now before us. And our discussion of these issues up to this point has rested on presuppositions about which there can surely be debate. It is time to step back from these issues large and small, and to raise a more general question about the fundamental nature and purposes of international educational and cultural affairs. A fresh look at first principles is in order.

5

Defining Educational And Cultural Relations

WHEN PEOPLE SPEAK OF "educational and cultural relations" be-tween nations, they speak in phrases whose scope is not easy to de-limit. In conventional usage, both "education" and "culture" have fairly narrow meanings. "Education" stands for any formal method of impart-ing to the individual something profitable or morally edifying; "culture" is the name for the fluffy spiritual dessert that people earn if they have first dealt successfully with the meat and potato realities of life. "Educa-tion" so conceived never stands for miseducation; and "culture" so understood never includes such things as baseball, poker, respect for timetables, or reverence for techniques of mass production.

Unless we are prepared to accept these genteel definitions of "edu-cation" and "culture," however, it is plain that these terms have a range of application that can be very broad. In its most general meaning, "education" refers to any experience or series of experiences that have an effect on an individual's subsequent character, beliefs, skills, or tastes. That dinner, that meeting, or that mistake, we say, gave us an educa-tion. Whether its effect was desirable or undesirable, it was still edu-cation. Fagin as well as Socrates was an effective teacher. "Culture" stands for what education, so conceived, produces—all the modes of behavior, preferences, ideas, and conscious or unconscious reactions to experience that are "second nature" to a man or a people, and that represent, so far as is known, a much larger component of human con-duct than the "first nature" that comes from genetic inheritance.

67

THE CONNECTION TO FOREIGN RELATIONS

When education and culture are conceived in this way, the educational and cultural relations between nations are not something special or set aside, but are an accompaniment of whatever other relations—political, commercial, military, or perhaps merely geographic—nations may have with one another. They are not a separate kind of relationship; they are a product of any kind of continuing contact between nations—and if the quality of human experience is the touchstone of value, they are the most important product. Thus, war has been a major form of educational relationship between nations. It has been a potent means by which the people of different nations have affected the experience, behavior, and outlook on life of people in other nations. The development and exportation of the mass-produced automobile has similarly been a major event in the educational history of twentieth-century nations.

Viewed in this perspective, "educational and cultural exchange" cannot be conceived as consisting simply of the movement across borders of students, scholars, books, and paintings. It includes the movement of tourists, businessmen, and soldiers, of movies, popular music, and machinery, of sales methods and military techniques; it also includes the movement back and forth across borders of spies, recriminatory propaganda, and attitudes of mutual suspicion.

But I do not dwell on the amplitude of the expression "educational and cultural relations" in order to prepare the way for the announcement that the subject of this study has suddenly been changed and has been extended to cover the whole field of international relations. There would be little intellectual profit in defining the subject so broadly. Before looking for a more manageable definition, however, it is useful to bear in mind that educational and cultural activities as usually defined —the kind of clearly labeled activity in which foreign ministries, ministries of education, learned societies, schools, universities, and religious organizations engage—are only a part, and a small part, of the educational and cultural commerce that nations have with one another. Definitions, precisely because they sharpen and delimit a subject, can also tend to separate it from its larger context and to make it the prey of vicious abstractions. The perhaps obvious point that a broad meaning can be assigned to the phrase, "educational and cultural relations" helps to set the issues and problems to be examined in the larger setting to which they belong. Some serious errors in the theory and practice of educational and cultural relations come from a failure to do this.

To take an important example, scholarly inquiry and bitter experience during the last fifteen years have made it increasingly plain that economic development cannot be viewed as a self-sustaining thing-in-itself. It depends on the existence or emergence of appropriate educational and cultural conditions, and it implies and causes educational and cultural changes. The export of machinery and know-how, or of tricks of marketing, publicity, and industrial organization, is more than merely "technical aid." These things carry with them implicit cultural attitudes toward inherited traditions, the nature and meaning of work, the definition of efficiency and social utility, and the relations that should obtain between professional groups, between social classes, and in everyday human intercourse. If this wardrobe of cultural attitudes, or another suitable one, is not picked up by the recipients of technical aid, the aid is likely to be ineffective, and may in fact turn out to be a source of disorientation, disorder, and frustration. In the countries affected, programs for technological change or industrial growth are commonly perceived and correctly perceived as programs for radical social, psychological, and moral change. If there is neglect of this truism by protagonists of technical progress, they will be unprepared to understand the problems they encounter.

More generally still, the broader use of the phrase "educational and cultural relations" calls attention to the fact that international relations today have changed in a fundamental way. The degree of communication between the populations of different countries has reached an extraordinary intensity and depth. Indeed, even when governments make a prodigious attempt to control and to distort and exploit the information about other countries that reaches their populations, the amount of attention they give to the issue indicates its importance. The American standard of living, for example, is a domestic issue in the Soviet Union. The educational and cultural aspect of international affairs, in brief, is more visible and significant than it has ever been before. One of the most distinctive features of the twentieth-century international scene—and the one that is central to the entire problem with which this study is concerned—is the degree to which the populations of different nations are exposed to massive educational influences emanating from other countries, the United States not least of all.

What government or any private agency can do in the area of educational and cultural relations is only to supplement or inhibit, color or discolor, a process that no government or private agency can either start or prevent. Just as no discussion of disarmament is realistic that does not explore the implications of the fact that scientific inquiry will go on and that military technology, therefore, is subject to radical alteration, so no discussion of educational and cultural affairs can be realistic unless it recognizes that *deliberate* exchange, the kind of exchange that is carried on with the conscious intent to exchange, is normally but a drop in the bucket compared to the exchange that takes place unintentionally and as a by-product of other activities. Unless this is kept in mind, impossible expectations are entertained, and unnecessary disappointments are courted. It is tempting for people in charge of formal exchange programs, public or private, to imitate Chanteclair, who thought that because the sun rose every morning when he crowed, he was causing the sunrise. But while it is tempting, it is also mistaken.

NARROWING THE DEFINITION OF EDUCATIONAL AND CULTURAL ACTIVITIES

Against the background of these observations, we may turn to the problem of finding a narrower and more workable definition of "educational and cultural activities." A cue to such a definition is offered by a common use of the word "education." "Education," in this use, stands for a process that has two salient characteristics. It represents a *deliberate and organized* effort to affect an individual's beliefs, tastes, or abilities. It is to be distinguished, therefore, from the more informal and often more powerful ways in which individuals come to learn things. Secondly, "education," in this use, refers to a process with long-range objectives. Its purpose is not to affect the individual's behavior for just this moment but over a long period of time, and with regard to a variety of situations that cannot be foreseen. This distinctive objective is a good part of what lies behind the common distinction between "education" and mere "training." It is supposed that the skills—for example, reading—the dispositions—for example, tolerance—and the ideas

—for example, that substances expand when heated—that one acquires through education are more broadly transferable from situation to situation, and more likely to affect the individual's basic outlook and character, than are the skills, dispositions, and ideas that one acquires, for example, in learning to drive a car or to take shorthand.

With this use of the word "education" in mind, "educational and cultural activities" can be more precisely defined. The phrase means first, activities, whether under public or private auspices, which are deliberately conducted for the sake of educational and cultural communication. Second, it means activities peculiarly concerned with long-range matters. Educational and cultural activities are conducted with one or more of the following purposes in mind: to impart or acquire skills and information; to affect or to enter sympathetically into the beliefs, attitudes, and concerns of others; to share with people elsewhere objects of enjoyment or admiration in one's own society or in theirs. The purpose of these activities is to impart or acquire information that is useful, not simply with regard to the events of the passing moment, but with regard to events over a much longer range of time; to affect beliefs, attitudes, and concerns, not simply in order to achieve some immediate goal, but to give them a more or less stable and enduring form; to share with others not simply the styles and fashions currently admired, but what have been, or seem likely to be, more permanent features of the cultural landscape.

So defined, educational and cultural exchange is not a by-product of other activities but a separate activity, which is conducted deliberately and for the sake of distinctive purposes. This definition excludes trade and business relations from the sphere of cultural exchange. On the other hand, it remains, quite intentionally, a broad one. It may well include commercial exhibits, the training of foreign personnel by American corporations, and information and propaganda activities.

Thus, much that the United States Information Agency does under the rubric, not of educational and cultural exchange, but of news and information, comes under this definition of educational and cultural activity. For the so-called "fast" media can have a long-range effect on the attitudes and perspectives of the audience to which they are addressed even when they restrict themselves to dealing with the passing scene, and this long-range effect can be a central objective of an information program. There is a penumbral area where "information" on one side, and "education and culture" on the other, fade into each other. Indeed, the fact that this definition points to the existence of such a penumbral area is one of the reasons for putting it forward. A definition which suggested that a sharp line could always be drawn would be blind to the realities. Nevertheless, even though there may be some overlapping at the border, a broad distinction between "educational and cultural programs" and "information programs" can still be drawn. There are significant differences in emphasis in the two kinds of program, in the character of many of the problems involved, and in the conscious order of priorities among the objectives sought. The interplay between "information" and "education and culture" is one of the principal themes of this study; the competition and collision between them is another.

HISTORICAL IMPERATIVES BEHIND GOVERNMENT ACTIVITY

The beginning of systematic thinking about policy in the field of educational and cultural relations lies in asking just what functions are served by the creation of formal agencies for the deliberate supervision or facilitation of such relations. An examination of this question may yield basic guidelines permitting a fresh evaluation of existing policies and practices.

1. The first imperative leading to the formal organization of educational and cultural affairs derives from the nature of intellectual work in the modern era. Although its most noted representatives are justly celebrated for their individualism and independence, modern intellectual work is an intensely cooperative enterprise. Communication with others is of the essence of responsible scientific inquiry. This is the imperative that led to the organization of scientific societies in the early modern era—the first large formal agencies, apart from the church, for the conduct of international educational and cultural relations. The requirements of communication are also a major reason for the exchange of students and professors, for this is an instrumentality, in the first instance, for communication between separate centers of research. Nor has the commandment, "Thou shalt keep in touch with thy colleagues," been accepted only by scholars in the natural sciences; it is accepted by social scientists and humanistic scholars in general.

Other characteristics of modern intellectual work reinforce the need for special attention to problems of communication, and add to the complications of these problems. One is the increasing speed with which new knowledge is accumulated. For purposes of economy, as well as of mutual stimulation and support, well-organized systems of communication are required. In addition, modern intellectual work has created a steady array of new, specialized disciplines, has encouraged considerable interdisciplinary cooperation, and is constantly moving into areas that fall between established fields of inquiry. In these circumstances, the normal professional societies are often insufficient as channels of communication. Coordinating committees, scholarly conferences, and the extension of personal contacts between otherwise isolated investigators are required to take up the slack.

These considerations apply, on the whole, to artists, musicians, and writers, as well as to physicists or geographers. Modern communication and travel, combined with the emergence, in most countries, of an educated audience whose tastes are international, have accentuated the long-noted tendency of artists and writers to interest themselves in each other's work. Today, French, Japanese, Mexican, and American writers, for all the special influences of their local environments and literary traditions, usually share certain books and writers as a common literary heritage—for example, Joyce, Proust, Kafka, Faulkner—and write not only for their compatriots but for one another. The spread of abstract expressionism, jazz, and aluminum-and-glass houses offers parallel evidence that the arts of painting, music, and architecture are international.

In both the sciences and the arts, in short, the existence of an international community is a fact, not an aspiration. To be sure, as in any other community, there are also cross-currents of local and tribal suspicion, conflicting interests, and sectarian prejudice. But elements of community remain. And this fact affects international relations and the calculus of power. Just as the growth of large-scale industry has created new demands for forms of economic organization that transcend national boundaries, so the growth of an international community in the arts and the sciences has created demands of which governments cannot help but be aware, whether they respond or not. Nor can any major government afford to turn its back on such pressures. For it depends on the active good will of the scientific and intellectual community in a way that governments in the past have not.

2. The significance for international relations of the emergence of an international intellectual community can be more fully grasped if another distinguishing feature of recent history is noted. Developments in technology have become the major generators of important changes in human society and in the international balance of power. The major source of these changes lies in basic scientific research in both the physical and social sciences. Every nation that wishes to be modern or that hopes to cope with the problems created by technological developments must accordingly rely on the active cooperation of scientific and technical experts.

The problem is technical, but it is also political and psychological. A nation must assure itself of an adequate supply of well-trained people, whether it finds them at home or abroad. In its own interest, it cannot be indifferent to scientific and technical developments elsewhere. There is, therefore, an urgent practical imperative for all nations to engage in international intellectual exchange and from a political and psychological point of view, governments must also concern themselves with international educational and cultural communication. The expert will do a better job for his country if he believes in what his country is doing; and he is helped to believe in what his country is doing when his country shows itself sensitive to his own particular occupational interests and concerns. In pragmatic terms, this usually means, among other things, that his government must permit and encourage active contact between him and his colleagues in other countries.

3. To stress the purely technical role of intellectual workers in modern societies, however, is one-sided, and can encourage a dangerous sort of error with regard to international educational and cultural policy. The modern "intellectual" serves another function as well. It may be illustrated by a story about Emil Lederer and Rudi Hilferding, two outstanding students of early twentieth-century mass movements, who had a conversation in a Viennese cafe in 1916 about the possibility of a revolution in Russia. Lederer was convinced that a revolution was coming, but Hilferding is supposed to have scoffed at him. "Who will make this revolution?" he is said to have asked scornfully. "Mr. Trotsky of the Central Cafe?" The Mr. Trotsky in question was Leon Trotsky.

It is not necessary to argue that all intellectuals are potential generals of revolutionary armies. But modern Western history, for two or three centuries, has been marked by a major shift in the social role of intellectuals. To some extent, this has simply reflected the growing practical importance of such fields as law, medicine, science, economics, and journalism. To a larger extent, it represents a consequence of the secularization of society and the spread of literacy. In any case, whatever the reasons, a major feature of modern history has been the rise of intellectuals to a position of pivotal importance in society.[1] As the role played by intellectuals in most of the emerging countries illustrates, this trend is an essential part of what is meant by the "modernization" of a society. "Never before," says de Tocqueville, analyzing the causes of the French Revolution, "had the entire political education of a great nation been the work of its men of letters, and it was this peculiarity that perhaps did most to give the French Revolution its exceptional character and the regime that followed it the form we are familiar with." [2] Whether this statement exaggerates the facts, it points to a conspicuous feature of the French Revolution. It is one that has marked most subsequent revolutions of importance, including those that are now going on.

[1] It would take us far afield to define the phrase "the intellectuals" with the thoroughness the subject deserves. Briefly, the phrase, as I use it here, refers to a social category, and says nothing about whether the people who belong to it have certain capacities (or incapacities) of mind. An "intellectual" is a man, first, whose principal occupation involves dealing with words or symbols at a fairly high level of complexity. (This is a relative matter. In countries where educational levels are low, the concepts of "complexity," and "abstractness" are naturally more relaxed. Merely being a university student can be enough, very often, to qualify one as an intellectual—a significant factor affecting the political influence of students in these countries.) Secondly, an "intellectual" is a man who concerns himself with issues of general public importance and addresses himself to people outside his own specialized field. Specialized knowledge in itself, therefore, is not enough to constitute a man an intellectual. The late Norbert Wiener, for example, was an intellectual not because he was a cyberneticist but because, from the standpoint of this specialty, he discussed "the human use of human beings." It should be noted, finally, that to be an "intellectual" is not entirely a matter of self-election. In every society, there are associations, cafes, periodicals, clubs, and cliques which are identified as "intellectual," and the fact that one has been admitted to them, though such admission may be a wholly informal affair, is part of what is normally meant by identifying a man as an "intellectual." Intellectuals are in this sense a reasonably definite social category.

[2] *The Old Regime and the French Revolution,* translated by Stuart Gilbert (Doubleday, 1955), p. 146.

The role of intellectuals, from this point of view, is not that of giving practical advice or supplying technical know-how. It is that of serving as a "censor-class" for the community. Located in the universities, the press, the theater, and the arts, the intellectuals, in almost all societies, are a major group from whom members of the educated and semi-educated publics draw their opinions about the character and moral quality of their society. It is often said that with the rise of an increasingly specialized and technical society, the significance of the intellectual as a general guide and critic is waning, and that his power in the future will be even less than it has been in the past. Such views overlook the peculiar role of intellectuals, which has relatively little to do with the practical advice they may give or their proximity to people in power.

The attitudes that the members of a society hold toward its reigning institutions do not depend only on their judgment of the efficiency of these institutions. They depend also on whether these institutions are in accord with their general *weltanschauung* and can be justified in a language that they regard as an appropriate language for discussing such matters. (Thus, relatively few Americans or foreigners find fault with American institutions on the grounds of their inefficiency; the more usual denunciation is that America is "materialistic." The very efficiency of American institutions seems sometimes, indeed, to be the reason for criticizing them.) In other words, the stability and strength of social and political institutions depends not only on their practical performance but on their symbolic *legitimacy*. To a considerable extent, the secular intellectuals of modern nations have supplanted the clergy as the principal suppliers and endorsers of the symbols of legitimacy. "Capitalism," "socialism," "freedom," "justice," "exploitation," "alienation," etc., with the special reverberations they now carry, are intellectuals' terms.

The significance of this for foreign policy is as great as it is for domestic affairs. Over the long run, a major nation's foreign policy is unlikely to succeed, or will, at any rate, become more costly and more completely dependent on violence and the threat of violence, if it loses the understanding and sympathy of intellectuals in other countries and in its own. Nor can a foreign policy make sense to intellectuals unless it makes sense to them in their terms. This is a process that requires not so much either a technical expert's or a publicist's defense of each specific policy decision, but a continuing discourse between intellectuals of different countries in which they learn how to talk to each other. The growth of effective communication among intellectuals is a major ingredient of international understanding; the division of intellectuals into rival camps that are out of touch with each other is a principal cause of international misunderstandings and animosities.

4. Another imperative that has led to the formal organization of educational and cultural relations is the rivalry of modern states in demonstrating their preeminence in scientific research, technical invention, and artistic creation. The rivalry is, of course, anything but recent. It dates back to the renaissance, and, on a large scale, to the mercantile era and the competition between states for military and economic advantage and for political prestige. This rivalry has taken the shape it has only because nations have been in cultural contact with one another. Intellectual and artistic workers, more than any others, have an international audience. Governments have not created this state of affairs, but it has been to their interest to exploit it. They have a long-standing interest in borrowing or stealing the best minds and technical achievements of other countries, and in advertising the achievements that have been made possible by the national way of life which it is their mission to superintend.

Probably, of all large countries, the United States, until the last twenty years, has shown the least official interest in this sort of cultural competition. Whatever the reasons may have been—the assumption that the advantages of the American way of life were self-evident, an indifference toward many of the activities, such as music, architecture, or higher mathematics, in which cultural competition takes place, the larger perspective of isolationism—these reasons no longer exist. As the entry of the United States into the space race with the Soviet Union attests, the United States apparently shares with the Soviet Union the assumption that a nation's success in scientific or technological competition demonstrates the vigor of its social order, and that such a demonstration is necessary to keep world opinion and the world balance of power favorable to it. For similar reasons, there has developed an official interest in showing American educational and cultural wares to the rest of the world. Accordingly, although the considerations that have led the United States Government to promote international cultural communication are not entirely the same as those that have impelled the intellectual and artistic communities to seek such communication, a certain mutuality of interest between government and these communities has come to exist.

5. Reinforcing these considerations is the change that has taken place in the techniques of public communication and in the audiences to whom public communications are addressed. As a result of radio, telegraph, television, and the like, large proportions of the populations of all countries live in a theater of experience that is international in its dimensions. The Congo, Vietnam, Alabama, and Baku are potentially anybody's business—or, at any rate, anybody's occasion for argument or for demonstration in the streets. Moreover, the spread of an egalitarian and democratic ethos has meant that policy-makers commonly address themselves, and try to make themselves intelligible and persuasive, to great numbers of people who are not themselves policy-makers but the consumers or victims of policy.

In the process, the governments of the world have become involved in efforts to speak over the heads of other governments, and directly to the populations of other countries. And in order to be understood and correctly interpreted, they must not only employ the "fast media" but must seek, through the "slow media," to create a more basic set of attitudes and understandings. They must therefore seek to employ such major channels for reaching populations as schools, universities, books, and the minds of influential opinion-makers. The growth of a formal government interest in educational and cultural affairs is a consequence.

This imperative is particularly strong in the case of the United States for a number of reasons. In the first place, the United States is itself a country in which, by tradition and habit, the government relies heavily on public opinion, and considers favorable opinion an important sort of justification of its policies. In the second place, the United States is a first-rank power with first-rank responsibilities. In the nuclear age, when the traditional threats of superior power lose much of their force, other instruments, such as an appeal to public opinion, acquire greater importance. Third, and perhaps most important, American technology and American culture—or the technology and culture of which the United States is a supreme symbol—are present almost everywhere, and are the causes or the symptoms of major changes in other societies. In other words, the United States is already in massive communication with other countries, even though much of it is of a nonverbal sort. It is probably the one country whose existence can never be forgotten no matter where in the world a man is.

This creates problems that affect the success of United States policy in manifold ways. "Development" is the kind of problem it is, partly because the countries involved are undergoing "development" under conditions in which the standards attained by developed countries—the United States first and foremost—are present before their eyes. And in Western Europe and Japan inevitable problems are created, with regard to the maintenance of harmonious relationships with the United States, by the fact that many members of these long-established and highly sophisticated cultures feel their inherited way of life threatened by the spread of American machinery, American techniques of organization, and American ways of doing things. An effort on the part of Americans to control the shape which the American cultural presence takes in other countries is a natural and a necessary response.

6. Finally, the role of educational institutions in the difficult process of economic and social modernization has become steadily more conspicuous. One of the most important new ideas that has emerged from attention to problems of modernization has been the idea of investment in human resources. Beyond this, the educational systems of all countries, developed or developing, are now called on to take up the slack left by the weakening of inherited institutions and social disciplines, and are under pressure to supply not only the skills, but the perspectives, ideas, and motivations that appear to be requisite to rapid but orderly adjustment to social change. It can be said with considerable assurance that educational institutions have never before been asked to do so much so quickly, nor has so large a proportion of every society's resources been so likely to be invested in them.

In sum, international relations have a technological and scientific setting, and an altered political and sociological context, which have pushed educational institutions, scholarly investigation, and the communications of intellectuals across the borders to the foreground of international affairs. Unless its universities, its scholarship, and its intellectuals reach out to other countries, fundamental domestic enterprises of a modern society will be seriously harmed. And if it fails to recognize the importance to its foreign affairs of its educational and cultural relations, it probably also ignores the factor which, as much as any, will affect its long-range destiny in the international arena.

6

A Tangle of Purposes

HAS THE RESPONSE by the United States government and by the American academic and cultural communities to the historical imperatives just discussed been effective? Has it been a response to central issues, or to side issues and superficial emergencies? We have reviewed the bureaucratic arrangements and disarrangements, the problems of communication between representatives of American and foreign cultures, and the trials and tribulations of Cultural Affairs Officers. But such a review gives us only a partial answer to these questions. Two other questions remain unanswered. First, what are the principal purposes that have guided the American response to the emergence of educational and cultural affairs as an important component of United States foreign relations? Second, do these purposes make sense?

Broadly speaking, four major purposes are conventionally assigned to the federal government's educational and cultural programs overseas: (1) the promotion of international good will and understanding; (2) the advancement of the objectives of United States foreign policy; (3) assistance in the economic and technical development of other nations; (4) the facilitation of scholarly and intellectual interchange, and the enhancement of educational opportunity for individuals. Around each of these purposes, pressure groups, constellations of interest, and official and semiofficial agencies have formed. In general, the sponsors of exchange-of-persons activities have stressed the first of these objectives; officials of USIA have stressed the second; AID has had the third most in mind; scholarly organizations have been most interested in the last. Debates about the policies proper to the field of educational and cultural

80

relations are basically debates about the relationship of these purposes to one another, and about which among them should have priority.

Is each one of these purposes, in itself, a defensible purpose? Does it rest on assumptions that are sound? Can it be translated into realistic action? When these purposes are viewed together, are they mutually compatible? Which, if any, is the most important? If policy in the field of educational and cultural relations is to achieve coherence and self-awareness, the accumulated conventions and presumptions of two decades of activity ought to be reexamined.

What follows is offered as a first step in this process of analysis and clarification. It is a process that requires, at many points, restating the obvious. But it is necessary to expose our basic ideas to the light of day if the existing tangle of purposes with regard to educational and cultural affairs is to be unraveled. In what is said, it should be understood, I am taking existing ideas about the purposes of educational and cultural relations as points of departure. I am neither rejecting them nor endorsing them. I am seeking to determine what general principles emerge from looking at them closely, and what inferences follow for the way one should think and speak about the basic objectives of educational and cultural activities.

PROMOTING INTERNATIONAL GOOD WILL AND UNDERSTANDING

The stated long-range objective of United States foreign policy, to which the nation is committed by a succession of public utterances from the highest level and to which an overwhelming majority of American citizens are undoubtedly devoted, is the creation of a peaceful world, respectful of diversity. To be sure, theoreticians and practitioners of international affairs sometimes dismiss such long-range goals as merely rhetorical, and as having little practical relation to the day-to-day pressures of foreign affairs. But the sentiments to which the long-range ideal of peace in diversity gives expression are undoubtedly sincere; and more to the point, the ideal expresses not only a distant goal of United States policy but one of its daily, practical, regulating conditions. From day to day, in the world as it now is, the United States cannot efficiently or peacefully protect its own national interests except by recognizing and respecting the different social conditions and cultural attitudes of other nations. Nor should the issue be put merely in terms of United States national interests. No civilized man loyal to humane ideals, or aware of the complexities and possibilities of the present century, can accept less than the goal of a peaceful world respectful of diversity. The ideal transcends national loyalties.

It may be taken for granted, then, that the promotion of "good will" and "understanding" among nations is a legitimate and necessary objective of United States foreign policy, and that its adoption is a matter of elementary prudence. And it is also reasonable to assume, in general, that programs to promote personal contact and communication among selected citizens of different nations are instruments that can further the achievement of this objective. To be sure, such personal contact and communication do not guarantee good relations between nations. Revolutions, wars, authoritarian governments, and powerful ideologies can intervene and destroy what such contact and communication have created, as past relations with Germany or present relations with China illustrate. However, while these examples are often brought forward to refute the belief in cultural exchange as an instrument of peace, it is reasonably clear that the breakdown of relations with Germany or China began with a breakdown of communication with people in those countries who had never had close relations with Americans or close knowledge of the United States. Bad will and misunderstanding are often encouraged by the simple fact that relations between the members of different nations are not immediate and personal, but vicarious and impersonal. In such circumstances, powerful stereotypes take over. "You don't know: you haven't seen," says the Chaplain in Shaw's *Saint Joan.* "You madden yourself with words." Educational and cultural exchanges that move people across the borders help them not to madden themselves with words. In this respect, there is solid warrant for the belief that such exchanges are important instruments for the promotion of international good will and understanding.

Yet, although this position is sound in its essentials, it is nevertheless useful to look at it with a hard and skeptical eye. For it is often surrounded by assumptions that reduce or destroy its validity. Thus, it is often assumed that "good will" and "understanding" are the same thing, or that they are as naturally related to each other as green grass and sunlight. But this is not the case. "Understanding" is an ambiguous term; when applied to relations between human beings, it sometimes stands for the growth of sympathy among them, but it also sometimes stands merely for their capacity accurately to describe and explain their fellows' attitudes and behavior. In this second sense, it is possible to understand another man without liking him. Indeed, it is possible to understand him and to recognize, precisely because you do understand him, that his interests and ideals are opposed to your own.

There is no ground for the common assumption, therefore, that the promotion of international understanding automatically promotes international good will. Many international animosities do have avoidable misunderstandings at their source and could be reduced or removed by better understanding. But this proposition is not universally true. If it were, the additional proposition would also have to be true that nations never have any objective conflicts of interest with each other. Even when United States policies are right, and even when others understand them, they may still not like them because they find them opposed to their interests. In fact, the hard choice often has to be made between promoting good will toward the United States and promoting objective understanding of the country and its policies. The rhetoric that lumps "good will" and "understanding" so easily together is agreeable, and is also dangerous, largely because it tends to obscure the presence of this everyday dilemma.

A second assumption, closely connected emotionally to the one that has just been discussed, is equally misleading. It is the idea that face-to-face meetings and personal association between people from different countries are the most obvious ways to engender sympathy and mutual accord. Astonishingly, this idea survives in the face of all the stories of abrasive relations between American tourists and their hosts in foreign countries. Nor is there strong evidence for the proposition that when people become more accustomed to the presence of foreigners, they are likely to be friendlier to them. In many areas that have long been Meccas for foreign visitors, the foreigner is ignored or regarded as a nuisance. In areas that have not known foreigners, the foreigner is often lionized.

Equally doubtful is the belief, which some seem to entertain, that close contact and sympathy between people of different nations is enough to keep them at peace. Undoubtedly, such contact and sympathy can act as a brake against the development of tensions that make negotiation and agreement difficult. Equally important, the development of objective understanding of the conditions and attitudes really prevailing in another country can prevent major miscalculations. Such miscalculations were made in Japan and Germany before World War II by people who did not know the United States at first hand. Nevertheless, nations that have been exposed to intensive face-to-face contacts with each other—for example, France and Germany—have also gone to war against each other.

These are all homely truths, and one would hesitate to repeat them were it not for the excessive statements that are frequently made about the relationship between educational and cultural exchange and the achievement of peaceful relations between nations. As in any other field, a certain folklore has grown up around educational and cultural affairs. The folklore is not entirely false; it is, in fact, more true than false. But it is imprecise and overly simple, and it can lead to disappointments unless the assumptions that constitute it are carefully qualified. Nothing that has been said is meant to imply that, on balance, the personal encounters promoted by intellectual and cultural exchange have not been useful in the cause of international understanding and good will. The evidence very strongly indicates the contrary.[1] Nevertheless, the objections that have been made to some of the folklore that surrounds educational and cultural affairs calls attention to the fact that in the planning of exchange programs, a number of safeguards and guiding principles are desirable.

To begin with, the obvious cautionary note is required that the people involved in exchange programs should be carefully selected and appropriately prepared. Specialized intellectual or scholarly abilities, while generally indispensable, are not sufficient to guarantee that an individual will be an effective participant in exchange programs. It seems likely, too, that those who have already engaged successfully in exchange programs with a given country will be useful judges of who should succeed them.

Secondly, the effort has to be made to avoid the scattering of limited resources. The assignment of people to places or positions where they will not be used to best advantage has to be prevented insofar as this is possible. Single-minded concern with the promotion of "good will" and

---

[1] See A *Beacon of Hope: The Exchange of Persons Program* (U.S. Advisory Commission on International Educational and Cultural Affairs, 1963).

"understanding," and optimistic assumptions about the automatic connection between exchange programs and these objectives, can divert attention from the importance of such elementary considerations. In general, it appears to be the mark of wisdom not to think of the objectives of exchange programs in such broad terms, but to attempt to work with more limited and definite objectives in mind. In general, exchange programs should be used to produce a *concentrated* and *continuing* effect with regard to *selected* educational, scholarly, or cultural objectives.

Finally, the conditions under which participants make contacts with people in other countries cannot be left to chance, but have to be reasonably well arranged. On the whole, experience suggests that Americans abroad or foreigners in this country have the best time, and contribute most effectively to the cause of good will and understanding, when they are required by their work and their environment to immerse themselves thoroughly in the local scene. This is perhaps the supreme lesson of the Peace Corps. When travelers come mainly as observers rather than as participants and partners in shared enterprises, they generally observe less and understand less; and their hosts return this compliment to them.

In sum, the phrases, "good will" and "international understanding," although they refer to legitimate and noble ideals, are not sufficient to serve as guides to well-constructed programs of educational and cultural exchange. The words are too vague to indicate what a reasoned program of action should be, and they do not provide criteria by which the success of educational and cultural programs can be adequately measured. Furthermore, too much confidence is likely to be placed in the idea that merely by expanding the volume of exchanges—without giving principal attention to who is exchanged, where he goes, what he does, and why he does it—the purposes of educational and cultural exchange will be promoted. Aristotle warned in his *Ethics* that men should not consciously seek happiness even though it is the goal of human activity. International "good will" and "understanding" appear to have the same relationship to human effort that "happiness" does. They are rarely achieved by direct assault. They are more usually by-products of activities in which men work together for other reasons that seem to them good and sufficient in themselves.

ADVANCING UNITED STATES
FOREIGN POLICY OBJECTIVES

When we turn from the promotion of good will and understanding to the second purpose conventionally ascribed to educational and cultural programs—that of promoting the specific objectives of United States foreign policy—it might seem that we have come down from the clouds to firmer ground. Government programs in educational and cultural affairs, however small they may be in comparison with military or technical assistance programs, involve large expenditures of public funds, and this money is spent in foreign countries or for the benefit of foreign nationals. Is there any justification for public expenditures for educational and cultural programs abroad if these programs do not make a positive contribution to the achievement of United States purposes vis-à-vis other countries?

The question need only be put into words and there appears to be an obvious answer. If we leave purely humanitarian consideration aside, there is no readily apparent reason, so long as the present system of sovereign states exists, the United States Government should spend money or use the energies and talents of any of its citizens in programs that do the United States no definite good. Comparisons with other countries fortify this conclusion. The example of the British Council is often brought up, for instance, to drive home the point that at least one major nation with much experience in international educational and cultural activities has chosen to separate these activities sharply from foreign policy and foreign propaganda. But while it is perhaps possible to make a case on pragmatic grounds for this way of organizing and conducting educational and cultural affairs, the example of the British Council does not touch the issue of principle which is under discussion. There can be little doubt that the British Council would be forced to "close shop" immediately if it were deemed by the Foreign Office to be working at cross-purposes to British foreign policy. It is, in fact, the cultural arm of the British Government overseas, and it is generally perceived as such by the citizens of the countries where it conducts its programs.

From such considerations, however, a particular conclusion is commonly drawn. It is that educational and cultural programs abroad are properly viewed as tools of the Secretary of State and the Director of the

United States Information Agency. There can be arguments pro and con, those who take this position may admit, about the most efficient way to employ these tools, but there can be no argument with the proposition that educational and cultural programs should be judged primarily in terms of their contribution to foreign policy. At this point, ideas emerge that are as much a part of the unexamined folklore of educational and cultural affairs as the ideas examined earlier under the rubric of "good will and understanding."

The first difficulty is that there is usually less precision than there should be in defining what is meant by "foreign policy." In its most normal signification, "foreign policy" stands for the decisions and actions—and, hopefully, for the principles behind these decisions and actions—that a government takes in relation to other governments. United States foreign policy, in this sense, is intended to produce certain pressures on other governments, or to induce or enable them to take certain actions, which are deemed to be consistent with the interests of the United States. Thus, NATO or the embargo on Cuba are parts of United States foreign policy in the usual meaning of the word. Economic assistance to other countries has often been commonly viewed in this light; and the operations of USIA are clearly intended to support foreign policy so conceived.

If this is what is meant by "foreign policy," however, and it appears to be what is usually meant, there is considerable difficulty in fitting educational and cultural programs within its framework. The relationship between the visit of a prominent American scholar to Athens and the Greek Government's decisions about Cyprus is dim; it remains dim even if the scholar happens to be a leading specialist on the Middle East. The likelihood that a successful tour in the Congo by an American jazz band will alter the balance of forces there is equally dim; when the claim is made that such a tour contributes to the purposes of the United States, those who make such a claim must have something other than immediate political purposes in mind. Advocates of educational and cultural relations as instruments in the building of international good will and understanding are not alone in holding some excessively optimistic views. Hard-nosed advocates of the position that educational and cultural affairs are merely a part of foreign policy also appear to hold such views.

Nor does the usual rejoinder to such observations save the case for using educational and cultural activities as tools of foreign policy so conceived. This rejoinder is that it is a mistake to look for immediate effects from all aspects of an information program and that certain of its aspects are intended simply to create an atmosphere favorable to American information programs and United States foreign policy. This, it is pointed out, is a process that takes time. Educational and cultural programs are ultimately intended to influence the behavior of other governments, but they are intended to influence not this year's government, or even next year's, but the next decade's. Precisely to the extent that this point is sound, however, it implies that educational and cultural programs cannot be judged by the same standards that apply to everyday diplomatic activity or the information programs attached to it. An effort to fit educational and cultural programs within the confines of an annual "country plan" is absurd and self-defeating.

For the essence of the rejoinder we are examining is that a sharp distinction should be made between short-term and long-term programs. The objectives of educational and cultural activities are educational and cultural. It is reasonable to assume that if they are successful, there will be better understanding in the long run of United States policy and a more favorable view of it. But it is not reasonable to assume that these long-range objectives can be achieved if American educational and cultural representatives abroad are also burdened with the task, from day to day, of promoting the short-term actions and policies of the United States Government.

The distinction between these two kinds of activity is sufficiently important to justify the creation of a vocabulary to take care of it. "Short-term" and "long-term" foreign policy or, perhaps better, "foreign policy" and "national policy" can be differentiated. The United States as a nation and a member of world civilization has an unquestionable interest in educational and cultural programs abroad. It has this interest in part because such programs contribute to a more favorable American "image" and make it more likely that United States political policies will succeed. But it has this interest as well because American educational, scholarly, and cultural resources can make an important contribution to the well-being and enjoyment of life of people elsewhere, and to the stability and peacefulness of their societies. And it also has this interest because other people's intellectual and artistic achievements are sources from which the United States can draw strength and guidance. In this context, international educational and cultural programs are tools of United States national policy. And only in this context does it make sound practical sense to say that these programs should be judged by their contribution to the national interests of the United States.

Even from the point of view of the immediate objectives of foreign policy, there are strong practical reasons for stressing the separation of educational and cultural affairs from the immediacies of diplomacy or propaganda. Secretary of State Dean Rusk is on record with the view, for example, that educational exchange programs make the best propaganda when they have no propagandistic purpose. The Department of State and USIA, furthermore, must concentrate much attention on crisis situations, present or potential. Their energies are directed in large part to problems of an emergency character. In such circumstances, the central business of educational and cultural programs can be neglected or distorted. Moreover, a too eager emphasis on the political purposes of these programs can discourage participation by artists, scholars, and students who come from private life, and can put American education and culture in precisely the wrong light by making them appear to be simply the servants of politics. In the eyes of most civilized men, the reverse is the appropriate relationship.

Equally important is the fact that we live in a propagandized world in which people have developed a certain capacity to resist propaganda, and are likely to be suspicious of it even when it is truthful. By and large, the evidence indicates that people generally listen to what they want to listen to. For this reason, United States information programs require the long-range support of educational and cultural programs. For the same reason, United States educational and cultural programs are weakened by close identification with diplomacy and propaganda.

An eminent Italian with many years of experience in international cultural activities, and with particular interest in Italo-American relations, put this point to me in this way:

> The American presence is very visible in Italy, but it is mainly the American business presence. Your contribution to the arts and sciences, and to the common civilization in which we Italians think we have a special proprietary interest, is not nearly so visible. You are, in a word, not fully or accurately represented here. And then, to make matters worse, you are constantly after us, trying to get our people and Government to support a multi-lateral force, or a broader scheme of European federation, or a vote against Communist China in the UN.

I understand, of course, why this has to be. But over the long run, our attitudes on such matters are formed less by the arguments you bring to bear on each individual case than by a general flow of sympathy. If that sympathy is to flow towards you we have to feel that you and we are contributing to the same civilization and share more or less the same values. You do not create this feeling if you cannot separate Italian culture from Italian politics, which is one thing today and another tomorrow. And you do not create this feeling if you seem unable to make this same distinction with regard to your own society.

It appears once more, then, that a commonly accepted purpose of the government's educational and cultural activities is misleading. A restatement of this purpose is necessary.

CONTRIBUTING TO ECONOMIC AND TECHNICAL ASSISTANCE

Economic and technical assistance is commonly regarded as a principal object not only of the educational programs conducted by AID, but also of programs for which CU is responsible. Just as is the case with the objectives of educational and cultural activities that have already been examined, it is difficult to quarrel with the proposition that economic and technical assistance to developing nations is in the interest of the United States and of world peace, and that American international educational and cultural activities ought to contribute to this end.

Nevertheless, the relation of American educational institutions to programs for economic and technical assistance has in practice often been very difficult. And in theory the role of the individual scholar, of learned societies, and of universities within the framework of such programs has not been clearly defined. Two types of confusion appear to be involved. The first has to do with the nature of the process known as "technical assistance" and of the broader process called "development." The second has to do with the special needs of educational institutions, needs which have to be met if they are to make an appropriate contribution to United States aid programs abroad. Taken together, these two sorts of confusion suggest that it is a mistake to conceive of educational activities abroad as part of technical assistance unless, once again, careful qualifications are introduced.

The nature of "technical assistance" raises the first issue. Despite the apparent hard-headed specificity of the term, it stands, in fact, for a highly artificial abstraction—for a process that takes place only in a much larger context of understandings or misunderstandings. So-called technical assistance is not likely to achieve its purposes unless it is culturally penetrative. For it to take hold and to stimulate the "take-off" it is intended to stimulate, the people in the societies receiving technical assistance must make appropriate changes in the ways in which they conduct their business or regard such elementary matters as work, productivity, the distribution of the national product, and the responsibilities of elite groups. Repeatedly, to take an elementary instance, programs of technical aid founder because people in key positions in host countries are more sensitive to their obligations to their immediate families than to their obligations to promote efficiency and a climate of opportunity. This is not immoral behavior in their eyes, but moral behavior; what is at issue is a conflict between moral systems, not a conflict between purity and corruption. Technical assistance, in a word, sets up conscientious resistances to it and encounters problems that are not technical but political, ethical, and anthropological.

Despite this fact, the educational component of United States aid programs is marked by an emphasis on the exportation of conventional American know-how, unsupplemented by any continuing intellectual dialogue that explores the larger issues that lie beneath the surface. It is not likely that Americans can go to other countries and give them advice, based only on American experience, which will help them solve the social and cultural problems incident to development. But it is even less likely that American technical assistance will achieve any great success unless Americans indicate, in some regularly established and continuing way, that they are aware that such larger problems exist and that they are disturbing and complex problems. The creation of conditions in which educational leaders and intellectuals in the United States and in the developing countries can maintain close communication, independently of specific technical assistance projects, would appear to be an indispensable supplement of effective technical assistance. And those who participate in this process of communication should include humanists, social scientists, and natural scientists, as well as engineers and specialists in educational administration.

A narrow view of the nature of technical assistance encourages still other mistakes. Although there is much attention in country planning

to economic development, there is less attention to political development. Despite the awareness of the problem's importance by officials at
the highest level in AID, there is also less than adequate attention, at
the operational level, to what has come to be known as "human resources development." In a country as large and significant as Brazil,
for example, there has been a long period in which no full-time education officer has been attached to the AID mission. And although directives have been issued in Latin America permitting the organization of
educational programs apart from specific economic projects, officials on
the spot report that these directives are in conflict with the basic instruc-
tions in their manual. In general, the concept of "careful country pro-
gramming" seems to leave little place for long-range educational planning. For the problems one faces when one tries to engage in such
planning do not fit easily into the categories employed by economists
and engineers dealing with specific technical problems.

As a consequence, educational assistance under AID has usually,
though not invariably, been "project-oriented." It has been conceived in
the limited terms appropriate to the accomplishment of a specific economic objective such as the building of roads or the establishment of
fisheries. It is closer to "training," in a word, than to "education." This,
in general, is a major consequence of unguarded statements to the effect
that educational and cultural activities should be conceived as instruments of technical assistance. A narrow view of technical assistance
narrows the scope of educational planning and the character of the
education attempted. In turn, educational and cultural activities are
prevented from playing their larger roles in the process of social development on which technical progress depends.

In 1962, Edward Weidner wrote of AID's predecessor, the International Cooperation Administration:

> Within ICA, education in the broad sense of the term has been
> lost. Education has had a narrow professional ring: teacher educa-
> tion, vocational education, audio-visual education, and the like. No
> one at a responsible level has ever been concerned with the broad edu-
> cational approach to technical assistance. Universities become occa-
> sionally used tools, nothing more. The same defect was evident in
> AID, as initially proposed to Congress. Planning, economics, com-
> modities, financial assistance, and development research all had rec-
> ognizable homes, but development education had none.[2]

There has been steadily more awareness of this issue in AID, and definite attempts have been made to deal with it. This verdict, nevertheless, continues to suggest the general trend so far as the relation between education and economic assistance programs is concerned.

A narrow view of the nature of technical assistance is also reflected in the second principal sort of confusion that affects the relationship of educational activities to economic assistance programs. To a considerable extent, the peculiar characteristics of scholarship and of universities—their special needs and resources, their style of organization, and their operating ethos—are misunderstood or ignored. Individual scholars and universities as institutions are habituated to large grants of independence, and require such independence, not only in working out their own answers to problems put before them, but in defining and selecting the problems with which they will deal. Their interest in issues, furthermore, is of a long-range sort. When they engage in practical projects, they normally require that these projects yield fruits from the standpoint of continuing theoretical inquiry.

In order to use scholars and universities to best advantage, therefore, a relationship should be constructed that emphasizes continuity over a reasonable period of time and that gives scholars and universities an opportunity, within broad limits, to design the form of their activities. Indeed, if education is accepted as a major ingredient of "development," there is good reason to advocate that planning for educational development be conducted with some degree of independence from economic or technical planning. Obviously, such planning cannot be entirely independent. Disaster is courted if educational plans are made without regard to the capacity of an economy to absorb the products of an educational system. But it is not the case that educational plans should merely fit economic plans. Economic plans should also take account of educational requirements, and these cannot be determined without the active participation of teachers, scholars, and educational institutions at the level where basic plans are made.

Among other things, such an approach to educational planning as a component of development might help prevent two harmful features of the present situation. First, the narrow emphasis on "technical" educational assistance generally means that a university that takes part in assistance programs is only very meagerly represented. Only a few mem-

² Edward Weidner, *The World Role of Universities* (McGraw-Hill, 1962), pp. 327-28.

bers of the faculty are aware of its activities, and among the great majority who are left out there are likely to be many who regard such international activity as an unnecessary frill. Second, the university is represented overseas in a distorted fashion. The place that vocational education plays in the larger scheme of American education will be misunderstood, and damaging stereotypes about American education will be reinforced. And the broader educational requirements of developing societies are likely to be ignored. There is no a priori reason why professors of literature or political theory should be less closely identified with educational development programs overseas than professors of public administration or veterinary medicine.

These considerations, which favor treating educational exchange as an instrument for educational development independently conceived, take on added force when the great demands being made on American colleges and universities are taken into account. A proper balance between service on the domestic and foreign fronts, the development of more adequate resources to meet the urgent needs that exist, and the economical use of the inevitably limited resources that will be available even if present resources are expanded, call for integrated planning in which scholarly organizations and universities themselves take a major part. The limited view of the role of scholarly organizations and universities that reduces them to the performance of ad hoc tasks is probably a source of considerable wastage.

In sum, it appears reasonable to conclude that one chief purpose of educational and cultural activities is to contribute to the economic and social development of other countries, and, it should be added, of the United States. But it is also reasonable to conclude that it is misleading to formulate this purpose in such a way that educational exchange is force-fitted to the needs of "technical assistance" narrowly conceived. Indeed, a reverse emphasis is probably justified. As J. G. Harrar, President of the Rockefeller Foundation, has observed:

> Friendly nations cannot resolve the fundamental problems of the less developed or emerging nations, but they can help to speed the processes of social and economic growth by collaborating in projects of readily demonstrable benefit that can be completed or ultimately transferred to local agencies. . . . The most basic consideration of all . . . is the extent to which each project can serve as a training facility for the nationals of the countries concerned. Only by emphasizing the training aspect of foreign assistance is it possible to develop per-

manent roots and to achieve continuity and multiple benefits from an enlarging force of competent personnel able to serve national needs.[3]

From this point of view, the largest single purpose of technical assistance is the advancement of educational objectives.

PROMOTING INTELLECTUAL EXCHANGE AND EDUCATIONAL OPPORTUNITY

The fourth purpose commonly assigned to international educational and cultural programs has the great virtue of appearing to make these programs their own justification. The pursuit of peace and of political and economic objectives, with all the complications they represent, recedes from view. Educational and cultural exchange is represented as a straightforward matter with its own obvious and unarguable objectives. Its justification is that it contributes to the progress of the sciences and the arts, and enhances the opportunities of students and scholars— both those who travel and those who stay at home—to improve their minds and extend their imaginations.

No free man or free government, surely, can oppose such an aim. A willingness to promote it, indeed, may be taken as one simple test of the degree to which a government is civilized. Moreover, it is the one purpose that must be accomplished if any of the other purposes of exchange programs—the promotion of good will, the advancement of the long-range purposes of United States policy, successful assistance to other nations seeking technical or economic improvement—are to be achieved. Unless knowledge is extended, unless literature and the arts are stimulated, unless individuals improve their skills and sensibilities, and unless such purposes are the ones they have in mind when they engage in exchange programs, the chance that the other broad purposes of exchange will be accomplished is slight. For they are generally by-products, in the context of exchange programs, of the successful pursuit of specific intellectual and educational objectives. From this entirely practical point of view, these objectives of exchange programs have an initial primacy over all the others.

[3] "AID Abroad: Some Principles and Their Latin American Practice," in F. Emerson Andrews, ed., *Foundations—20 Viewpoints* (Russell Sage Foundation, 1965), pp. 42-43.

Yet, primary though these objectives may be, it is self-deception to believe that they can be pursued in isolation from other purposes. In the narrowest terms, scholarly and cultural interchanges require attention to extraneous matters that are not intellectual in character but that can make the difference between the success and failure of a program—for example, adequate housing and schooling for children. Beyond these, there are differences in language, in the structure and mores of university systems, in ideas of physical comfort. Concentration by participants in exchange programs on common professional problems can do much to overcome such difficulties, but they cannot be erased. Somebody has to worry about them and take deliberate steps to deal with them. Educational and cultural exchange therefore requires an administrative apparatus, and other than purely scholarly or intellectual skills are required to keep exchange going. The right people have to be recruited, and the right arrangements have to be made for them; in the process, people with skills as travel agents, linguists, contact men, educational planners, and diplomats are indispensable.

Nor do such considerations do more than scratch the surface of the issue. Scholarly styles and interests that seem natural to people in one society—for example, mathematical methods in the social sciences—may seem unnatural and even threatening to people in another society. The protocol of classrooms, the examination system, the rules of the professorial tribe, can puzzle visiting students. The attitude toward athletic competition encountered in a foreign country can provoke not the interest but the consternation of a visiting hockey team. Ideas about the uses to which the theatres of a country should be put can arouse the indignation or sense of superiority of a touring dramatic group. These are merely symptoms of the broader issues affecting the educational and cultural commerce between nations.

No matter how strong the professional interests that bring people from different countries together, they meet as people from different cultures. A special effort or a special talent for understanding is required that is not required when people from the same culture work together. Moreover, the historical relations between nations, their adventures and misadventures with each other, have an effect on the relations between individual members of these nations. Without doubt, individuals can rise above these questions and meet as individuals; when they do, their relationship is likely to have a special warmth and poignancy. But that does not alter, it rather reinforces, the general proposition that, whether we like it or not, we live in a politicized world in which communication between members of different nations tends to have political overtones and political meanings.

The conduct of a continuing and successful program in international educational and cultural relations requires that attention be given to more, accordingly, than the immediate problems of professional communication and cooperation. It requires attention to these processes as they take place in the larger context of foreign affairs, and it requires the creation of conditions under which members of the intellectual and artistic communities of the United States and other countries can conduct a continuing discourse, not only about purely professional problems, but about the more general problems affecting their capacity to communicate and cooperate with each other. In these circumstances, to say that the sole and sufficient purpose of educational and cultural exchange is the advancement of scholarly, educational, and cultural objectives is to risk over-simplification. However important this purpose, it cannot be pursued in a vacuum. This conclusion is further strengthened when the urgent need for co-ordinated planning is taken into account. The proper husbanding of resources requires programs that concentrate on specific and definite intellectual or cultural objectives, that have continuity of impact, and that are rigorously selective with regard to the goals to be sought. The planning of such programs with regard to any specific nation inevitably demands attention to ancillary but significant issues such as the nation's attitude toward and understanding of American culture, its political orientation, and its economic and social aspirations.

It is interesting to speculate what the consequences would be if the federal government were to support international educational and cultural activities as ends in themselves. It may be taken for granted that the government cannot and should not oppose the free movement of ideas and of people across borders. But leaving out practical political or economic considerations—the promotion of good will, the furtherance of United States foreign policy objectives, the giving of technical assistance—why should the federal government actively support and facilitate this movement? There would appear to be only one reason, at any rate if we leave altruistic considerations aside. It would be as part of a general commitment to support and improve education and research in the

United States. American international educational and cultural programs would then be a part not of foreign policy but of general educational and cultural policy.[4]

Whether such a state of affairs would be better or worse than that which now prevails is something of which no one can be sure, but it would be different. It would involve a drastic reorientation of educational and cultural programs in certain respects. They would come under the aegis, presumably, of the Office of Education, or of such agencies as the National Science Foundation, a National Humanities Foundation, a National Arts Council, or the National Academy of Sciences. And a good deal of what is now done for its effects in foreign countries might be curtailed or eliminated. But even if such a radical redirection of existing organization and policy were to take place, most of the issues we now confront would remain. The movement of students and scholars would go on, the dialogue—or should one say the broken dialogue—between American intellectuals and their foreign counterparts would remain an issue, development programs overseas would continue, and so would diplomatic and information activities. The directors of the government's educational and cultural programs might have a new angle of vision on these matters, but they would still have to take them into account.

In brief, the obvious purpose of scholarly and cultural interchange is scholarly and cultural interchange. But this is not a sufficient guide to policy.

---

[4] The consequences for American education and research that our interest in the developing world has already had are discussed in "The Non-Western World in Higher Education," *The Annals of the American Academy of Political and Social Science*, Vol. 356 (November 1964). Of special relevance with regard to the contributions of the federal government is the article, "The Federal Government and the Universities," by Kenneth W. Mildenberger.

7

A Restatement of Purposes

IF WHAT WAS SAID in the last chapter is defensible, existing ideas about the purposes of the federal government's educational and cultural activities abroad still leave something to be desired. The purposes commonly ascribed to them—the promotion of international good will and understanding, the advancement of the objectives of United States foreign policy, assistance in the economic and technical development of other nations, and the facilitation of scholarly and intellectual interchange—point, in a general way, to reasonable and desirable goals. But these goals need to be stated with greater circumspection and sharpness if policy is to be more orderly and precise and if public discussion is to be more pertinent to the actual nature, possibilities, and limitations of educational and cultural programs.

How should the purposes of American educational and cultural activities abroad be formulated? The discussion in which we have engaged supports a restatement of these purposes, I would suggest, under five main headings: (1) the lacing together of educational systems; (2) the improvement of the context of communication; (3) the disciplining and extending of international intellectual discourse; (4) international educational development; (5) the furthering of educational and cultural relations as ends in themselves.

LACING TOGETHER EDUCATIONAL SYSTEMS

International "good will" and "understanding," though laudable objectives, are vague and hard to measure and are subject to the accidents and vicissitudes of domestic and international politics. They point in

99

the direction, however, of a more precise and tangible goal—the lacing together of the educational systems of different countries. The analogy of trade relations is a useful one in thinking of the purposes of educational exchange. When societies are tied together by extensive commercial relations and are economically interdependent, there is no guarantee that they will not come into conflict with each other. But a practical deterrent to runaway conflict has been constructed, and modes of cooperation have been created that may survive the ebb and flow of emotions and events. The potentialities of educational and cultural cooperation in this direction are probably even greater than the value of trade relations. As yet, however, these potentialities have hardly begun to be tapped.

Over the long run, it can make a great difference to the relations of the United States with other countries, and to the cause of international peace, if the teachers and scholars of other countries have a close familiarity with American activities in their fields of interest, if they have had experience in the United States as students or teachers, if they know their American colleagues personally and remain in touch with them, and if the conferences, and text-books, and footnotes that constitute the substance of educational and scholarly affairs reflect intensive communication with American scholarship and education. And the reverse relationship—the use by Americans of the work of their colleagues abroad—is equally important. For the process here envisaged, needless to say, is not the "Americanization" but the internationalization of scholarship and education.

In such a long-range perspective, a habit on the part of foreign teachers and scholars of turning to American books and periodicals in conducting their work has more practical significance than that they should call themselves "pro-American" or regularly approve the actions of the United States Government abroad. The phrase "international community" is a slippery one that lends itself to sentimental rhetoric. It begins to take on substance when, in a major sector of life of all nations—the educational sector—habits and institutions are developed that make for shared transnational interests, common perspectives, a common fund of information and ideas, and a practical system of mutual dependence.

This restatement of one of the purposes of international educational and cultural exchange has practical implications for policy. To take an example, the hope behind programs in "American Studies" has been to increase the understanding of the United States as a center of culture and civilization.[1] But this is to treat American culture and civilization as a particular branch of learning; and, in other countries, it will necessarily be a branch at a distance from the main trunk of learning and of interest mainly to specialists. It will not have the same relationship to the main corpus of study that mathematics, physics, economics, or major fields of history will have.[2] A conception of educational exchange as an effort to lace educational systems together throws the issue into a different perspective. It suggests that the problem is to connect American scholarship and culture to the main trunk of scholarship and culture elsewhere, and that a more promising way to do this would be to stress matters of central educational and intellectual interest in other countries, and particularly those matters with respect to which Americans can make a special contribution—for example, English-language training, or instruction in the special methods of social research that have been developed in the United States.[3]

[1] For a more detailed study of programs and problems of American Studies, see Walter Johnson, *American Studies Abroad*, a special report from the U.S. Advisory Commission on International Educational and Cultural Affairs (July 1963).

[2] The role of American studies in a total program of educational and cultural exchange will be examined later.

[3] A similar approach would also be indicated for cultural presentations. Less attention would be given to the presentation of "Americana," a type of presentation that often reinforces rather than reduces foreign stereotypes about the United States, and more attention would be devoted to the contributions the United States is making to common international enterprises in the arts, music, or drama. Thus, in selecting a play for presentation, the leading questions to be asked are the following: Is it, as a result of its style, theme, or manner of performance, likely to stimulate *sustained* discussion among theater people and critics in the country visited? Is it likely to promote continuing contacts between professional theater people in the United States and in this country? Does it, above all, have a chance to make a difference in the history of the local drama? The reported impact of the American musical, *West Side Story*, in Japan, or the impact of "the theatre of the absurd" in the United States are examples that meet these tests.

Some striking efforts illustrative of these principles have already been made. For example, a story in the *New York Times*, June 24, 1965, reports: "A New York theater group headed by Harold Clurman, here to participate in a new kind of international collaboration in the performing arts, has left in triumph after giving an informal and unplanned presentation of Eugene O'Neill's 'Long Day's Journey Into Night' for selected audiences. How well the experiment succeeded will be seen when a Tokyo company does the same play in September for the general public in Japanese, which will be the culmination of the Clurman experiment. The Clurman group

It would be reasonable to explore the hypothesis that an effort directed toward lacing educational systems together is more likely to achieve definite results than an effort whose conscious purpose is simply to promote friendly feelings. As with any other educational or cultural purpose, the accomplishment of this purpose will, of course, take time; an expectation of quick results is incompatible with it. But it is a purpose that is not grafted on to the other purposes of teachers and scholars; it is simply an extension of the natural interest of the best teachers and scholars in what is going on elsewhere, and it proposes merely to make it easier and more rewarding for them to follow that interest. Moreover, in speaking of an effort aimed at "the lacing together of educational systems," I am speaking of something more definite than "good will." Success or failure, with respect to such an effort, is more easily measured, and if success is achieved, its consequences will be more enduring.

IMPROVING THE CONTEXT OF COMMUNICATION

A second major purpose of educational and cultural affairs may be described as the improvement of the context of communication. What I mean by this phrase may be illustrated by an adventure I had a number of years ago as a Fulbright professor in France. At the request of the American Embassy, I was giving public lectures on American philosophy at Lyon and Grenoble. At the end of one of these lectures, I found myself in conversation with a schoolteacher, an intelligent and

had been here about three weeks, demonstrating to the Komo Gekidan Company of Tokyo how Broadway goes about putting on a major play, from the first reading of the script to the final rehearsals. . . . Mr. Clurman and five associates were brought to Japan for the project by the United States State Department as part of its cultural affairs program in foreign countries. Every day, on a stage in a rented hall, Mr. Clurman went through all the motions of a director getting a new cast into shape. . . . The purpose of the whole enterprise . . . was not to give a thrilling evening to a selected group but to impart something of top New York theater technique to serious Japanese show business."

So far as the major countries are concerned, there is a fairly large movement of books, plays, and works of art, not to mention the immense movement of movies, magazines, and the like. Government-supported programs, which, at best, provide a minor complement to these proceedings, should aim at the kind of exchange likely to attract the serious interest of key audiences and to leave a continuing result behind it. (Perhaps needless to say, there are some reasonable exceptions to this rule.)

friendly lady in her middle years. She told me how interested she was to learn that Americans, too, were interested in philosophy and went on to say that it was a source of constant surprise to her to learn how broad and varied American intellectual life was. Then she remarked, with a mixture of curiosity and diffidence, that there were certain things about America that puzzled her more than ever, now that she was coming to understand the country better. I asked her for an example. She replied, with an obvious effort to be kind, "Well, you have the custom of putting sugar on your steaks. Forgive me for using the word, but it is barbarous. At any rate, it seems that way to us."

I was taken aback, and said to her that while I knew that there were Americans as well as some people from other countries who put sugar on their steaks, this was by no means a custom of our country, and was in fact an exceptional occurrence.

"Ah, no, but everybody does it!" my interlocutor persisted.

Knowing that she had not been to the United States, I asked where she had read about this interesting custom. By now she was as puzzled as I. "I haven't read about it," she said, "I've seen it in the movies."

I think she saw from my face that I was sinking fast. At any rate, she went on, mercifully, to explain: "In your movies, one sees people going into restaurants, or truck drivers going into what you call 'diners,' and they sit down and order steaks. And one sees them eat the steaks, and always there is a sugar bowl on the table."

"But that doesn't mean they put the sugar on the steaks," I expostulated, and then I realized what the problem was. In France, the sugar or condiments that are to go with a course are brought to the table when needed, and taken away after being used. In the United States, they are often left on the table whether they are used or not. The lady had made an automatic inference, and, given the customs of her country, a logical inference, from the facts before her.

Communication between cultures involves this elementary problem. To enter into a culture is to be able to hear, in Lionel Trilling's phrase, its special "hum and buzz of implication." In one society, one thing signals another thing; in another society, it does not. People may be unaware of this system of signals and cues, but because they share it, they understand each other, often without having to put their understanding into words. This is in good part what it means to say that people have a common culture; at a simpler level, it is why old friends who have shared many experiences are likely to feel particularly close to each other, and to communicate in something like a special code. And if we are unaware of the unspoken codes that other people use, we are likely not to understand them or to misunderstand them. Moreover, to the extent that we are unaware of our own code, we shall have trouble making ouselves clear and plausible to them.

A primary purpose of educational and cultural exchange is to become aware of others' cultural codes and of our own—to bring to the surface the context of unspoken facts and assumptions within which their words and actions, and ours, can be correctly interpreted. It is an elementary and well-recognized truism that people elsewhere do not look at things from the same perspective Americans do. But it is perhaps not so well recognized that this problem cannot be overcome by direct methods of persuasion, and only partially by abstract lectures on American life, politics, or economics. For in speaking to others, Americans make assumptions these others do not make, and, in listening, others make assumptions that Americans do not make. This is a problem that affects most international communication.

The specialized languages of science and of formal diplomacy are the results, each in its own way, of more or less successful efforts to deal with this problem. But in an era of mass communications, mass movements, and democratic sentiments, the problem has taken on new proportions, and constitutes one of the basic reasons reasonable relations between nations are difficult to achieve. The insistence that an effective information program requires educational and cultural activities as an adjunct represents, though somewhat dimly and distortedly, a recognition of the existence of this problem.

To some extent, a better context for communication can be created, to be sure, by direct measures. It is impossible to understand the problem of Negro rights in the United States, for example, without understanding that the United States has a federal system, and that the term "United States" is the name of a continental nation of extraordinary diversity of tradition, outlook, and circumstance. Similarly, it is hard to explain the way in which American institutions of higher education maintain standards unless people are aware of the role of semiofficial accrediting agencies and of the wholly unofficial, but very well understood, system by which universities are rated. It is in this context that "American Studies," in the interdisciplinary form in which they are normally presented, serve their primary function. They provide general information calculated to eliminate major kinds of misinterpretation.

To say this, however, is not to restore American Studies to the position which, a little earlier, it may seem that they were denied. They have an important function, but it is not quite the function, when seen in this context, that they are too often given. It is not to persuade or to be a show-case of American achievements; it is to promote a correct understanding of the United States and a relevant interpretation of its policies. In foreign affairs in general, and in educational and cultural affairs in particular, it is probably less important to the United States that the behavior of others toward it be governed by approval of Americans than that it be governed by accurate knowledge of them.

As here envisaged, "American Studies," in broad terms, would fall into three major categories. (1) The interdisciplinary programs in American Studies, which cause so many complications when efforts are made to fit them to academic patterns elsewhere, should probably be ad hoc affairs aimed in the main at nonscholarly audiences such as journalists, budding civic and political leaders, and trade-union officials. Such programs should be tailored to the specific needs of specific audiences and specific countries. (2) More long-range efforts should normally fall within definable disciplines so that they can strike roots in established departments and can lead either to the broadening of basic programs of study to include American materials, or to the establishment of continuing programs of specialized study that will have the full respect of the academic community involved. (3) Special seminars and conferences, which bring together American and foreign students or scholars, should be addressed not to American themes as such, but to problems, disciplinary or interdisciplinary, that are of mutual concern and present opportunities for cooperative inquiry. Studies of political federalism, urbanization, the comparative roles of intellectuals, and the relation of the mass media to the fine arts are only some of the examples that come to mind. Needless to say, these recommendations should not be followed where they collide with established programs that have demonstrated their success. In building for the future, however, they may offer some useful guidelines.

Nevertheless, it would remain a mistake to expect programs in American Studies, however constructed, to carry the main burden of an effort to eliminate the static and the dead spots that interfere with international communication. Generalizations about a culture are helpful; they are also often overly simple and misleading. Understanding another culture is a matter of understanding a vast variety of things in a vast variety of specific contexts. It involves catching innumerable cues and signals that do not lend themselves easily to explicit statement or formal codification, and that often appear bare and unimportant when, apart from their immediate contexts, they are stated or codified. There is no adequate substitute, in short, for personal exposure to a culture, and for the reports that those who have been successfully exposed bring back. And not the least value of such exposure is that the awareness of the special characteristics of one's own culture may be enhanced. This is a major reason why emphasis should be given, in programs of intellectual and cultural exchange, to the movement of people, and to the placing of these people in positions in which they will be participants to some degree in the going enterprises of another society.

DISCIPLINING AND EXTENDING INTERNATIONAL INTELLECTUAL DISCOURSE

It would greatly oversimplify the harsh complexity of most international conflicts, and it would ascribe more influence to intellectuals than they have, to say that international conflict has its source in the quarrels of intellectuals. Nevertheless, there is a kind of devious truth in this statement. International affairs are peculiarly susceptible to galloping abstractions—"Communism," "Africa," "Imperialism," "the Free World." Nowhere else do massive stereotypes and personified ideas play a larger role; nowhere do they do more to rigidify disagreement, to give it a quality of necessity and higher nobility, and to turn otherwise manageable conflicts into unmanageable ones. And intellectuals, more than most other groups, have the power to create, dignify, inflate, criticize, moderate, or puncture these abstractions.

The character of international conflict, in other words, is influenced by the language that comes to be used in public to explain what is going on, to justify the positions that are taken, or to negotiate disputes.

The quality of this language is something that intellectuals can do much to affect. This is a fundamental reason for thinking that the presence or absence of habits of disciplined discourse between the intellectuals of different nations has much to do with the chances for the rational resolution of international conflicts. The promotion of such disciplined discourse is, or should be, a principal purpose of educational and cultural activities.

In speaking of "the disciplining" of international intellectual discourse, I mean, first, the gradual tempering of the stereotypes that affect intellectual as well as popular analyses of world affairs. Personal contact between the intellectuals of different nations tends to undermine the organized fantasies that grow up when such contacts are missing. Given the right conditions, and given a reasonable effort on the part of intellectuals to make sense to each other, such personal contact encourages the qualifying of generalizations, and the recognition of the differences of opinion that exist within national groups. If these contacts are maintained on a continuing basis, they can also exercise a countervailing pressure against intellectual, political, and bureaucratic inertia. As the relations between the United States and the Soviet Union over the last decade illustrate, there is a notable tendency in international affairs to persist in analyses and policies after the facts have changed. Vested interests, intellectual and practical, which have piled up around the old analyses, conspire to produce this result. The promotion of close association between the intellectuals of different nations can discipline discourse in the simple sense that it can help bring it closer to the complex and changing facts.

Closely connected to the criticism of stereotypes is a second objective designated by the phrase "the disciplining of discourse." This is the creation of opportunities for kinds of discourse that will encourage intellectuals in different countries to speak to each other rather than past each other. A good example of existing difficulties is offered by discussions of "democracy." In approaching this theme, American scholars, as often as not, are unconcerned to discuss ultimate questions about the basic meaning and validity of democracy, a system whose character and justification they take for granted, and prefer to discuss more technical questions about its actual workings. A larger percentage of foreign intellectuals, in contrast, are interested in debating definitions and ultimate ideals. The issues, in consequence, are never quite joined, and discourse is frustrating. Other subjects illustrate the same difficulty. In a symposium on cities, an American will discuss traffic problems; a German will discuss "urbanization and alienation." In a discussion of "modernization," an American will approach the subject as though it were morally neutral; a Japanese will insist that it cannot be defined except in evaluative terms.

I hope, in offering these examples, that I am not myself contributing to the rigid stereotypes I earlier deplored. Obviously, the differences are not absolute, but are matters of degree, and neither all Americans nor all foreigners conform to the generalization that has been offered. But this, in fact, is just the point. International meetings, publications, and formal educational and cultural exchanges can be used to strengthen and extend the capacity of American and foreign intellectuals to address themselves to the same subjects at the same level of discourse. One way to do so is to select themes for joint and continuing discussion and study that have been carefully limited and defined. The localization of issues by intellectuals, and the development of a vocabulary for discussing such limited issues that avoids the great conflicts of ideologies, can pave the way for new forms of international cooperation with regard to such issues.

Such a disciplining of international discourse would be unlikely to succeed, however, if it were not accompanied by an attempt to engage in international discourse on larger, ideal themes. The historical character and moral significance of the radical changes taking place in twentieth-century civilizations are any civilized man's concern. It is *not* clear that men can discuss them without sharpening the ideological disagreements that separate them. It *is* clear that even men of thorough reasonableness and good will cannot be expected to come to the same conclusions about them. But it is also clear that when men do not talk to each other about these questions, they are not likely to understand each other very well.

Plainly, there are limits to what should be attempted. When individuals are known to be nothing but spokesmen for fixed, dogmatic, and officially consecrated outlooks, there is not much point in asking them to take part. If they can be expected to speak as representatives of their nations rather than as individuals, they will be out of place.

And if they are intellectual wheelers and dealers seeking intellectual bargains and mergers, they will also be as out of place as if they partici- pate only to engage in polemics: they will cast doubt on the honesty and integrity of the proceedings. For the object of such confrontations is to allow men to face other men who see things differently, and to talk with them, in a friendly spirit, as clearly and responsibly as they can manage. It is not to attain agreement or to win approval for the policies of one's country. In the long run, it is less important to see eye to eye with others than to seem to be interested in the kinds of questions in which they are interested, and able and willing to discuss these questions with them.

The absence of this sort of dialogue—and only this sort of confron- tation, personal, continuing, responsive, and rigorously intellectual, deserves to be called by that word—is one of the principal factors that has adversely affected the relations of the United States with Latin America. The maintenance of such a dialogue is probably necessary not only to better relations with the countries to the south in this hemisphere, but to programs of economic assistance in most parts of the world, and to the easing of the misunderstandings and irritations present in American relations with Western Europe, Japan, India, and other countries. The possibility of using international meetings, periodi- cals, and certain specific assignments under American exchange programs with this central purpose in mind is worth exploring.

DEVELOPING INTERNATIONAL EDUCATION

It is against the background of the three purposes that have already been described that the contribution of educational exchange to pro- grams of economic and social development can probably best be understood. Even when educational exchange is approached from the point of view of economic and social development, it should not usually be viewed as a means to an external end—economic and technical assistance—but as an instrument, in its own independent terms, of *educational* development. As has already been said, complete independence from economic projections and possibilities is of course undesirable. But the most important job that educational institutions can do in foreign-assistance programs is to aid in the development of educational institutions. That is what they look best doing, and that is what they can do best.

There is a strong case, therefore, for establishing educational planning and development on its own feet both institutionally and intellectually. Universities and scholarly organizations, which have special needs and special goals, must enjoy considerable institutional autonomy in performing their functions at home. In performing their functions abroad, they also need a large measure of such autonomy. While they cannot think about educational plans for a given country in disregard of its political or economic circumstances, they should be regarded as equal partners in the planning process, with a perspective of their own that is as important as any other.

If these generalizations were to be put into practice, they appear to have certain specific consequences. First, it would probably be desirable to establish a sharper separation between the "hardware" aspects of foreign aid and the educational aspects, and to raise the latter to at least equal authority with the former. Second, it would be desirable to review the present educational practices of assistance programs that are largely "project-orientated," and to determine whether these should be classified as "training" (and therefore essentially ancillary to the "hardware" aspects of technical assistance) or, more broadly, as "education." Third, it would be necessary to ask, in each case, in what sort of general *educational* context such training programs were most likely to have the desired effects.

In such a reorientation of purposes, a presently neglected task of educational exchange with developing countries would probably emerge more clearly into view. Economic and technical development provoke —and require—social and psychological disturbance. Moreover, the process of economic development in most emerging countries, even when it leads fairly quickly to a rising standard of living, also invites the expansion of expectations beyond the possibility of immediate gratification. At one and the same time, people must be taught to conceive of a higher standard of living and to believe that it is possible to achieve it, and must also be taught that they must themselves work harder than ever, give up many of their accustomed pleasures, and postpone, for an indefinite time, reaping some of the material rewards of these sacrifices. Unavoidable though it may be, this is to scatter psychic gunpowder in a society. To control such situations, a strong ideology or sense of civic purpose is necessary, and also a belief, on the part of the people affected, that they know what is happening to them and why it is necessary.

The role of the schools in this context is of obviously major importance; it is all the more important to the extent that one has democratic values, and wishes to stress education as against the cruder and more manipulative techniques of mass persuasion. Allowing for some important qualifications, this major need of developing nations—a need for intensive and widespread programs in civic education—has on the whole been overlooked in AID assistance programs, although CU has been aware of its importance. Nowhere, possibly, could American educational institutions play a more important role. Obviously, they cannot merely export, unmodified, the courses in "civics," or, more broadly, in political science, economics, etc., that have been employed in schools and colleges in the United States. The success or credibility of some of these courses even in the United States, much less elsewhere, is problematic. But that such programs are needed is evident; and it is possible that a dialogue between American and foreign scholars might help produce such programs. In any event, an effort to do so might well be central to programs associated with educational development.

Finally, in speaking of "educational development" as a central purpose of educational exchange, it should be emphasized that I am speaking not only of the educational development of other countries, but of American educational development as well. The exposure of a considerable number of teachers, as a regular part of their careers, to experience overseas means a change in the attitudes and perspectives prevalent in American classrooms. A central and continuing commitment of central faculties of a particular university to overseas educational development means that, in this university, the international environment of the United States will be vivid. Indeed, it may be a parochial error that service by educational institutions in foreign fields necessarily means a drain on resources that would otherwise be available at home. Ideas, techniques, and experience from abroad, and foreign students and teachers, enrich American educational resources. If foreign service came to be regarded as a usual opportunity in the career of a large number of teachers and scholars, it is possible that more good people, not fewer, would wish to take up educational and scholarly careers.

FURTHERING EDUCATIONAL AND
CULTURAL UNDERSTANDING

No statement or restatement of the purposes of international educational and cultural activities would be complete, however, without adding what ought to be obvious, but unfortunately has ceased to be so. The pursuit of truth, the sharing of cultural achievements, and the effort to bring together the knowledge, collective experience, and imagination of mankind to improve the human condition are all enterprises that transcend the particular purposes of particular nations. Free trade in the arts and sciences, the free movement of people and ideas across borders, the free association of individuals with one another as individuals and not as members of different nations, are supreme achievements that are not to be justified politically. Political systems acquire their justification in large part from the contribution they make to these ends.

So long as the federal government makes a large investment in international educational and cultural activities, it is necessary and inevitable that these activities will also be measured by other purposes as well. But the most important of all issues is that the appropriate calendar of purposes not be turned upside down in the process. Educational and cultural relations are important, in the end, because they are educational and cultural relations. Fortunately, although there have been quarrels with this principle and distortions of it in the history of the federal government's involvement in international educational and cultural affairs, the principle has generally prevailed. Its central place in any defensible policy will have to continue to be borne in mind.

8

Variations on a Theme

THIS DISCUSSION OF EDUCATIONAL and cultural affairs has moved through three principal stages. We have discussed the problems encountered in the conduct of these affairs, particularly as they are seen from the vantage point of the man in the field—the Cultural Affairs Officer; the administrative conditions and the larger political and social setting in which these problems emerge; and finally, the theory of educational and cultural relations—their nature, their historical context, the imperatives that have called them into being, and the purposes by which they ought to be directed and judged.

Can these general principles be applied across the board, however, in a world whose essence is variety? Do the differences between the various regions in the world call for significant variations in educational and cultural policy? Discussion of this question must of necessity be brief, but this study would be incomplete without it.

Broadly speaking, the countries with which the United States has educational and cultural relations can be divided into three main groups: (1) those whose political and economic systems are reasonably similar to those of the United States and whose scholarly and educational establishments are highly developed—for example, Western European countries, Australia, Canada, New Zealand, and Japan; (2) the countries of the developing world; (3) the countries of Eastern Europe, particularly the U.S.S.R. Finally, the relation of American efforts in educational and cultural affairs to the work of international organizations, for example, UNESCO, must be considered.

113

RELATIONS WITH DEMOCRATIC AND MODERNIZED COUNTRIES

With respect to the countries in the first category, no special modifications of the principles that have been outlined appear to be necessary. It is probably true, of course, that with regard to these countries, less emphasis will be placed on what this study calls "educational development." Even this fairly obvious principle, however, cannot be pushed too hard. The special intellectual contributions that we Americans can make to scholarship in this or that European or Pacific or Asiatic country, and the special contributions it can make to us, should always be given high priority in the planning of exchange programs. In general, particular attention should be devoted to activities conducive to cooperative scholarly endeavor in areas of central intellectual importance.

Beyond the immediacies of exchange programs, however, there is also the problem of the general tone of such programs. So far as relations with Western Europe, Japan, and the other countries in this category are concerned, the most important imperative is to present American intellectual and cultural life as a free and independent phenomenon, with a continuity and durability unaffected by temporary changes in the American political climate or in the fortunes of the United States in the international arena. In Western Europe and Japan, there is an immense American "cultural fall-out." It presents, on the whole, the most restless and go-getter aspects of American culture. As far as possible, exchange programs and cultural presentations should be planned and conducted in such a way as to help put the picture of American culture in a less distorted and inconstant perspective.

To help achieve this goal, and simply in respect for the facts, the common traditions the United States shares with Western European countries should probably be stressed. A distinguished American professor of French is as useful, from this point of view, as a professor of American literature; and the professor who can present American literature in its relation to European literature, past and present, is to be preferred to the man who cannot. And in relations both with countries with a European tradition and with Japan, the effort should be made to choose themes for discourse and for intellectual cooperation that revolve around the common problems shared by highly industrialized liberal democracies in the current era.

Finally, the truism is perhaps worth reiterating that cultural relations involve a capacity to hear what others are saying and not only a capacity to speak one's own piece. While this particularly true in relation to the emerging countries, it is also true in relation to the richer countries. An overly eager approach to the business of persuading others can be self-hypnotic. It can generate so much noise that one cannot hear the sounds coming in the other direction. To hear those sounds is a major function of cultural relations, as of all other divisions of sophisticated diplomacy.

RELATIONS WITH THE DEVELOPING COUNTRIES

It is conventional to make a sharp distinction between the tasks of educational and cultural affairs in the so-called developing countries and in Western Europe and Japan. But while there is, of course, a difference in emphasis, a sharp distinction is in error. Educational and cultural relations between highly developed countries are most effective when they are conceived in terms of coherent, long-range plans, and when the central, conscious purpose of such plans is to increase the intellectual resources of the individuals and nations participating. Conversely, programs of "technical assistance" are likely to be effective only insofar as they are part of, and in themselves stimulate, a much broader process of cultural contact and communication. And the process must be two-way, for the donors of aid surely have as much to learn about what they are doing as the recipients. Indeed, a categorical distinction between "educational exchange" and "technical assistance" is not only invidious, but encourages an unduly narrow view of "technical assistance." The arguments against such a view are in general the same as those against a narrow trade-school education for the professions. In basic respects, therefore, the process of educational and cultural intercourse with the developing nations, so far as general principles go, is not different from the process of exchange with developed countries.

Some special factors, however, must be noted. Educational planning in developing countries must of course pay greater attention to economic projections and possibilities than is the case in more highly industrialized societies. To produce large numbers of people educated beyond the level of the jobs available is an obvious danger, and one that can easily materialize in many developing countries. Such people have the same effect on their societies as exposed nerve ends have on the body. In developing societies, too, a delicate balance has to be struck between the needs for education in the countryside and the needs in the cities. The acquisition of an education, or the desire for it, tends in all societies to draw people away from the country to the cities. In developing societies, this process, unless controlled, can aggravate the imbalance between town and country, which is one of these societies' fundamental problems. In educational relations with such societies there must also be greater emphasis on education at primary and secondary levels. The problem of balancing the needs of primary and secondary education against the needs of higher education, which exists in all societies, is also more acute in the so-called new nations, and mistakes carry heavier penalties.

Moreover, the problem of educational planning in the developing countries has some special practical complications. A prerequisite for effective planning, whether for education or for the economy, is the presence of appropriate administrative and political conditions such as a well-staffed civil service, reasonable assurance about the shape of the political future, and a measure of trust and cooperation between contending factions. Despite the training, intelligence, and high sense of devotion of many of the leaders of the developing countries, one cannot visit these countries and talk to their officials without recognizing that they cannot presuppose such conditions, but, at best, are in the process of creating them. It is in this respect that educational and cultural relations with the developing world differ most strongly from relations with the richer part of the world, and are likely to require special administistative and political skills. Obviously, too, flourishing cultural relations with these countries call for linguistic skills and for kinds of cultural information that are in short supply. The United States has been running steadily behind in finding people competent to perform the tasks required. The use of funds under the National Defense Education Act, and the recruiting of Peace Corps graduates for positions of higher responsibility in the areas with which they have become familiar, offer two possible ways to reduce this shortage.

To mention such problems, however, is also to call attention to one of the latent but important functions of educational and cultural relations with the nations of Africa, Asia, and Latin America. Such relations, when they are efficacious, involve not only the training of citizens of these countries by Americans, but the training of Americans by citizens of these countries. Intensive educational and cultural contact with these nations can be a contribution to American educational and scholarly development, repairing American knowledge of the world and American attitudes toward the world at their weakest points.

Over the long run, the impact on American primary and secondary education could be considerable. Latin-American intellectuals commonly point out, for example, how few Americans have ever had courses in Latin-American history in school, and how widespread are certain illusions in the United States, for example, the popular misconception that Pancho Villa was simply a bandit. The public opinion that makes for sensible foreign policy is not built out of such legends. Nor is it only with regard to the enlightenment and broadening of public opinion that intensified educational and cultural relations with the developing world make sense. The entire subject of "development" offers professional students of human behavior an unprecedented opportunity for systematic inquiry, and contains potentialities of considerable significance for the evolution of the social sciences. The emergence of area studies since World War II has been one of the most notable developments on the American educational and intellectual scene. It has already changed the character of much that is taught and studied in the social sciences, and has increased the insights for the understanding of American society and culture. And although no one can know, it may eventually have as much significance for the progress of human knowledge as the spectacular discoveries that have been made in the natural sciences. These achievements and potentialities derive in large part from the intensified process of intellectual and cultural exchange with the developing societies that has marked the years since the war. In sum, it is not inappropriate to use the word "assistance" in connection with American educational relations with the developing countries, but the assistance to American education and scholarship is part of what should be kept in mind. Just as in the case of American relations with the more developed countries, the educational and cultural benefits run in two directions.

RELATIONS WITH THE SOVIET UNION
AND THE EASTERN BLOC

Relations with the countries of the Eastern European bloc, and particularly with the Soviet Union, obviously present different problems from those encountered either in cultural relations with the nations of the West or with emerging countries of the Third World. The peculiarity in these relations is due only in part to the tensions of the cold war. For while the reduction of tensions that has occurred in recent years has been at once signalized and accelerated by the growth of cultural contacts between the United States and the U.S.S.R., stubborn difficulties remain. These stem, in the main, not from political rivalries, or even from the suspicion and hostility inherited from the past, but from the persisting and radical differences that exist between an open and a closed society. Nowhere are these differences likely to cause more thorny problems than in the area of intellectual and cultural relations.

As readers of this study do not need to be informed, the view has prevailed for many years in the Soviet Union that art, science, and scholarship are instruments of the state and its policies. Although Soviet intellectuals, artists, and scholars have recently begun to demand more independence, their struggle has gone on largely within the framework of this ruling presupposition. (Indeed, even though those demanding greater independence have been partially successful in achieving what they want, the degree of independence they seek would seem very small to most Western intellectuals.) Moreover, an analogous presupposition is applied to Western intellectual and artistic activity as well, which is regarded as a projection of "capitalist" reality, just as Soviet intellectual and artistic activity is a projection of "socialist" reality.

Soviet representatives are explicit in saying that while they believe in "peaceful coexistence" between states with different social systems, they do not believe in peaceful coexistence at the ideological level. In the Soviet-American Citizens' Conference held in Leningrad in the summer of 1964, in which I was a participant, and in every private conversation that I had in Leningrad and Moscow with Soviet officials and intellectual leaders on the subject of educational and cultural exchange, this principle was courteously but firmly reaffirmed. Political and bureaucratic controls, accordingly, are bound to be intrusive factors in educational and cultural relations with the Soviet Union, and cannot be wished away merely by an exercise in good will. In the circumstances, it might well seem that genuine intellectual exchange, particularly in touchy "ideological" areas such as the social sciences, literature, and philosophy, is impossible.[1]

Certainly, the obstacles that have been encountered are considerable, and an unusual combination of patience, ingenuity, insistence on principle, and sheer physical endurance on the part of negotiators for the State Department and for American scholarly organizations has been necessary to reduce them even as much as they have been. In general, the Soviet bureaucracy has adjusted itself slowly to the entire phenomenon of cultural exchange. To take some not unrepresentative examples from the period up to 1964, a scholar requesting permission to study contemporary Moscow dialect has been turned down on the ground that there were insufficient facilities for conducting such research. Another scholar, requesting permission to study Soviet agriculture, was turned down on the ground that he could find the information he wanted by studying Mr. Khrushchev's speeches. American students in the Soviet Union have encountered restrictions on travel, difficulties in obtaining materials from archives, and occasional harassment from police. American scholars, universities, and learned societies that have attempted to communicate directly with Soviet scholars whom they have wished to invite to the United States have often waited unreasonably long periods of time before receiving an answer, and have not infrequently received no answer at all.

Last but not least, there has remained the constant problem, in dealing with the Soviets, of "front groups." Soviet organizations ostensibly established to facilitate cultural exchanges commonly turn out to be instruments of Soviet political policy whose main concern, with regard to the United States, is to encourage the growth of parallel organizations in this country serviceable to Soviet objectives. Indeed, although these organizations are sometimes camouflaged as "private," many are overtly official.

These difficulties, which derive in part from Soviet administrative habits, and in part from the Soviet commitment to a political and

[1] These observations apply to the Soviet Union's allies, but with significantly less force to certain of them. It is perhaps superfluous to add that relations with Yugoslavia, which is not an ally of the Soviet Union, are not under discussion in this section.

ideological interpretation of cultural exchange, are enhanced by others that have independent origins. Copyright laws and other arrangements normally governing intellectual relations between different nations are often not recognized by the Soviet Union. The American and Soviet educational systems, furthermore, are differently organized. Research in the United States is carried on in universities; the most important scientific research in the Soviet Union, in contrast, goes on in institutes. In consequence, a Soviet scholar assigned to an American university will have a chance to observe and participate in the work of American laboratories, while an American scholar assigned to a Soviet university is less likely to have such an opportunity. Genuinely reciprocal exchanges, in these circumstances, require intelligent administrative discretion, rather than the mechanical application of labels and rules. Whatever the reasons, intelligent administrative discretion has not been conspicuous on the Soviet side.

Nor are these the only factors that have played a part in impeding the realization of even the modest goals for the exchange of students and scholars laid down in the agreements between the United States and the U.S.S.R. In both countries, military and quasi-military considerations adversely affect the free exchange of scholars in certain fields. In the United States, there remains an undertow of suspicion toward people who are able to communicate with Communists too easily, and there are also fears of "industrial espionage." In the Soviet Union, there is an incomparably wider, and apparently indefinitely stretchable, definition of "espionage," and there are much more profound anxieties about ideological contamination. Moreover, the Soviets do not have the same general range of interests with regard to scholarly exchange that Americans have. They appear to be mainly interested in scientific and technical areas, and they leave an unmistakable impression that they are more interested in studying American achievements than in allowing Americans to study theirs. Although they claim that it is the Americans rather than they who, on principle, bar certain fields of scientific investigation from the exchange program, the fact remains that they have repeatedly nominated people to do research in the United States in these affected areas, but have used the argument of "insufficient research facilities" to deny parallel requests by Americans.

For all these reasons, and they are weighty, cultural relations with the Soviet Union and Eastern Europe have been treated by the United States Government as *sui generis* and have been entrusted to a special office—the Office of Soviet and Eastern European Exchanges—in the Department of State. Despite the exhausting negotiations in which representatives of this office have engaged, progress has been spotty. Particularly with regard to the exchange of students and scholars, the agreements that have so far been made contemplate the exchange of only small numbers of people, and even these limited quotas have not been fulfilled in practice. Nor have representatives of the American Council of Learned Societies or of the Inter-University Committee on Travel Grants, a private, scholarly organization associated with the Soviet exchange program, had notably greater success in dealing with Soviet authorities. These disappointments cannot be laid at the door of those who have conducted the negotiations. They are the consequences of massive psychological, social, and political differences over which negotiators as individuals can exercise as little control as they can over the tides or the weather.

Yet this sobering recital of the record tells only part of the story. For the very character and magnitude of the difficulties that have been described provide the measure both of what has been accomplished in the field of Soviet-American cultural relations and of the importance of further efforts to extend these relations. The results achieved by negotiators up to the present time may seem unduly small to the inexperienced outside observer. They are in fact considerable accomplishments when the obstacles that have had to be overcome are taken into account. The very agreement by the Soviet Government to formalize and consolidate cultural relations with the United States is in itself a major departure in Soviet history. There has also been practical progress in the implementation of the agreements that have been made. For example, although there have been ups and downs in the process and uncertainties still exist, travel arrangements for American students in the Soviet Union have improved over the years, material in archives has been made more easily available, and disagreeable incidents with the police have diminished in number.[2]

---

[2] The most well-known exception, of course, is the arrest of Professor Frederick Barghoorn in 1963. For the record, however, it should be noted that he was not present in the Soviet Union under the exchange agreement.

Moreover, beyond the comparatively limited area of student and scholarly exchange, notable successes have been achieved. The Voice of America can now be heard in the Soviet Union. Technical and cultural exhibits have reached hundreds of thousands of people. Useful areas for scientific co-operation have emerged. Tours of the United States by groups like the Bolshoi Ballet or the Moiseyev Folk Dancers have not only given great pleasure to many Americans, but have generated at least temporary good feeling, and have probably helped to lessen the aura of strangeness and mystery that has for so long been attached to Russians in the American mind. Tours by American artists in the Soviet Union have probably had a similar effect. At the very least, they have given Soviet citizens a larger exposure to artistic variety and difference than they have had in the past. On all levels, this progress is significant. The general movement of American and Soviet citizens across the borders of the Soviet Union has increased enormously; and officials of the American Embassy in Moscow now see more Russians in a month or a week than, ten years ago, they saw in a year.

Despite the frustrations that have attended the cultural-exchange program, then, there can be little doubt as to its value. Indeed, although not all of it has worked out in accordance with expectations, its larger consequences probably exceed the modest expectations with which it began. Simply in increasing the number of contacts between Russians and Americans, and in making these contacts more customary and less strained, it has helped to open up the channels of communication. It has been associated with, and there is reason to believe it has accelerated, an important change for the better in the international atmosphere and in the posture of the Soviet Union toward the non-Communist world. In this judgment of the cultural exchange program, most students of the Soviet Union, and most people responsible for the practical conduct of relations with that country, from Ambassadors, Political Officers, and Cultural Affairs Officers to leaders of scientific and scholarly organizations, appear to concur.

At the same time, however, this discussion highlights the point that it is not possible at this time to isolate cultural relations with the Soviet Union from the larger questions posed by the relations of the two societies. Eagerness to expand cultural relations with the Russians has not, in the past, led to indiscriminate agreements with them, and should not be permitted to do so in the future. The essential issue is not that the United States must prevent the Soviet Union from acquiring significant technical information unless the United States receives similar information in return. Although this issue cannot be ignored, it is subordinate to, and part of, a more basic principle—that cultural exchange is not a competitive but a cooperative process, which cannot have desirable consequences if either side is trying to take advantage of the other. It is in terms of this principle, rather than in terms of the rivalry between the two societies, that such issues as the exchange of technical information should be discussed.

In terms of this principle, too, every effort should continue to be made to expand contacts in the arts, the humanities, and the social sciences. Central attention should be given, in this connection, to improving and enlarging the program for the exchange of individual scholars and students, which produces the closest and most durable forms of association, and which is the heart of the cultural exchange program in the view of most of those who have anything to do with it. Attention must constantly be given as well to improving the general context in which intellectual and artistic exchanges take place—the movement of books, newspapers, periodicals, tourists, and the like. Basically, it is important to press for the kind of unrestricted, unpolitical, and undogmatic intercourse that meets American intellectual standards. Progress toward such a goal must necessarily be step-by-step. Insistence on its validity should be a regulative principle of American policy.

From the immediate practical point of view, the principal question raised by this discussion is whether the program of cultural exchanges with the Soviet Union should continue to be administratively separated from the main body of American educational and cultural activities. The Office of Soviet and Eastern European Exchanges deserves the major credit for the progress that has been made in Soviet-American cultural relations. Particularly in the formative stages of the exchange program, it has probably been indispensable. While never relenting on matters of principle, and while always insisting on true reciprocity and on the keeping of agreements that have been made, the Office has striven energetically to open the channels of exchange between the United States and Eastern Europe. Although some American scholarly organizations, particularly among physical scientists, have complained from time to time at the obstructions interposed by this Office, the verdict of most scholarly organizations that have been closely associated with the Soviet-American exchange program is that, far from being obstructive, the Office has been of considerable assistance in facilitating communication with Soviet scholars and intellectuals and with the Soviet bureaucracy.

Nevertheless, despite the special problems presented by cultural relations with the Soviet Union and other countries in Eastern Europe, the arguments for continuing to administer these relations separately are overbalanced by the arguments against continuing to do so. It is true that American cultural relations with the Soviet Union and its allies in Eastern Europe are conducted under agreements that are separate from those governing relations with other countries, and are different in substance and spirit. On a deeper level, it is true that the conception of a nonpolitical relationship between scholars, writers, and artists belonging to different social systems is not in accord with Communist conventions of thought, and that, as a consequence, the Soviet bureaucracy, and the official organizations to which Soviet scholars and intellectuals are bound, stand in between American and Soviet citizens, and interfere with free relations between them. But this does not support the conclusion that special bureaucratic arrangements on the American side are the best means for reducing this evil.

The Board of Foreign Scholarships and the major scholarly organizations in the United States are aware of the special problems affecting relationships with the Soviet Union. Now that the program has been launched and a body of experience has been accumulated, there is no evidence that they need more than the usual forms of governmental assistance and protection in dealing with these problems. Administrative separation of the exchange programs with the Soviet Union breeds separateness in tone and in fundamental ideas about the purposes of American cultural activities. It gives a higher political coloration to American exchange programs with Russia when it is precisely the point of these programs to demonstrate the possibility of intellectual openness between two societies despite the political differences between them. The ultimate object of cultural exchanges with the Soviet Union is to create cultural relations with that country not significantly different from those maintained with other countries. Distant though this goal may be, the best way to move toward it appears to be to place cultural exchange with the Soviet Union under the same general auspices as the rest of the United States Government's cultural exchange programs.

A second practical question, though of less importance, also deserves attention. In my discussions with Soviet scholars and intellectuals, they repeatedly made the point that if government bureaucracies could be circumvented, and if they could make direct contact with American scholars about the problems incident to the exchange programs, many sources of irritation would be removed and the effectiveness of the program greatly improved. I am aware that the Soviet bureaucracy would not necessarily permit direct contact just because the United States bureaucracy was receptive to such an arrangement. I am also aware that the position taken by these people is congruent with recent Soviet proposals for changes in the exchange agreement that would permit "private" Soviet cultural organizations to negotiate directly with private organizations in the United States. It is perhaps unnecessary to add that I do not find myself overwhelmed by the conviction that private organizations exist in the Soviet Union.

Undoubtedly, the record of the United States bureaucracy has not been faultless. As the Soviets claim, there have been some delays on the American side as well as on the Soviet side in the processing of applications, the granting of visas, and related matters. It would be surprising, too, if Soviet rigidity, political and bureaucratic, had not provoked some counter-rigidity. Nevertheless, there is an element of innocence or of disingenuousness in the easy lumping-together of "government bureaucracies," Soviet and American. The controls exercised by American officials are not the same as those exercised by Soviet authorities. The comparison is tenuous between a bureaucracy whose activities are public only when the ruling party chooses to make them so, and a bureaucracy that must deal with an autonomous scholarly community and that is constantly under public pressure and criticism.

These considerations, however, should not prevent an effort to meet the overtures from Soviet scholars halfway. Considered as a specific proposal, and not as part of a general revision of the principles incorporated in exchange agreements with the U.S.S.R., there are good grounds for experimenting with the idea that established American scholarly organizations that are unimpeachably nonpolitical in character—for example, the American Council of Learned Societies, the Social Science Research Council, the American Academy of Arts and Sciences—might establish more direct links with Soviet scholars in an effort to simplify and ease some of the administrative difficulties that have attended the exchange program. This is not to propose, so long as present administrative arrangements exist, that these organizations replace government offices, or act in any way to dilute the authority of these offices. It is only to suggest that additional lines of communication should be made more readily available.

In judging the merits of such an approach, it is relevant to bear in mind that Soviet scholars and intellectuals are not a monolithic group, and that the evidence is increasing that some of their leaders are restive under the tight controls that are exercised over them. There is also evidence, if the conversations that I and others have had with them have any substance, that more of them than in the past are aware of the damage that has been done by front organizations and by the political manipulation of intellectual and cultural communication. In these circumstances, an affirmative, though frankly experimental, response to requests for the expansion of direct contacts with scholars and intellectuals in the United States appears to be desirable. If scholars and intellectuals in the Soviet Union are prepared to use such contacts for the purposes of scholarly and intellectual exchange alone, and if they are permitted by their government to do so, cultural relations with the Soviet Union would be greatly improved.

Obviously, however, one must assume that the continued improvement and expansion of cultural relations with the Soviet Union is desirable. Indeed, the entire discussion in this section of cultural relations with the Soviet Union rests on this assumption. Is it a sound one? The present discussion would be incomplete if it did not make explicit the reasons for maintaining that it is desirable to expand cultural relations with the Soviet Union to the full extent possible.

It is, of course, obvious that the leaders of the Soviet Union made their original decision to enter into formal cultural relations with the United States as part of a general program they thought of advantage to the Soviet Union. On the other hand, the truism is equally obvious that the United States can make no agreements with any major Power if that Power's leaders are not convinced that such agreements are to their interest. If Soviet leaders, through agreements with the United States, are encouraged to seek peaceful solutions of disputes and modes of international behavior that are of mutual benefit to the two societies, there is every reason to seek such agreements. And these considerations are particularly strong in the case of cultural exchange agreements. The individuals and groups in the Soviet Union that are most committed to moderate policies also appear to be those most strongly in favor of closer cultural contacts with the West.

Admittedly, open societies, in some respects, are more vulnerable than closed ones. The expansion of cultural contacts with the Soviet Union carries certain risks. American front groups may be encouraged and strengthened. Technical information the Soviets can use against the United States in the rivalry between the two societies may become more readily available to them. Outright espionage may become easier. But in the long view, such risks appear to be worth the cost. Front groups and the existence of technical information that is readily available and exportable are inevitable phenomena, in any case, in an open society. The expansion of cultural relations with the Soviet Union is not likely to add to the dangers implicit in them to a great degree. As for espionage, any gains the Soviet Union is likely to make in this direction are likely to be outbalance by the greater knowledge and understanding that the United States can gain, without benefit of spies, by the further opening of Soviet borders to American citizens.

In general, the rule of thumb seems reasonable that in a relationship between a closed and an open society, a change that makes the closed society more open is to the advantage of the open society. (In the long run, one cannot help but add, it will do no harm to the closed society either.) Even if the most pessimistic assumption is made—that closer and more frequent contacts with Americans will not in any way moderate the views of Soviet citizens about the supreme reasonableness of their own system or its eventual world-wide triumph—it is of the greatest importance to us and to them—that they come to realize at first hand that most Americans are unconvinced of the truth of these views, and are still neither fanatics nor fools. Nor is it less important that more ordinary Americans come to incorporate into their daily habits of mind the realization that there are a reasonable number of Russians who also refuse to fall into one of these two categories. Cultural relations between the two societies have the minimal function of converting the discourse that goes on in each society with regard to the other from mythological to naturalistic terms.

But there is no reason for making the most pessimistic of assumptions. Neither extreme pessimism nor extreme optimism is called for. It has already been demonstrated by the cultural exchanges that have taken place that Americans and Russians, if they try, can find issues that they can discuss usefully and rationally, and with respect to which they can find limited but important points of agreement. Such honest exchanges of opinion, free from ideological recrimination, are not likely to lead either many Americans or many Russians to wish to change places with people on the other side. Nor can they be expected to remove all the antagonisms between the two societies. But they help to correct stereotypes, to bring abstract formulas a bit closer to the ambiguous facts, and to build a habit of discourse and a language for discourse that make mutual toleration and accommodation more possible.

The effects with regard to the evolution of Soviet society that may follow from the further expansion of cultural relations with the Western world should also be taken into consideration. The opening of Eastern Europe to freer intercourse with the West has already had noticeable consequences; even in the Soviet Union, where the windows to the outside world have been opened the least, the consequences appear to be substantial. The response by ordinary Soviet citizens to such aspects of the American exchange program as the graphic arts or communications exhibits, as well as the response of many Soviet intellectuals to the opportunity for freer exchange, reveals that the appetite for contacts with the West has been increased rather than appeased by the contacts that have taken place. It is an appetite that should surely be encouraged if the process of intellectual de-Stalinization is to be accelerated. An enlarged program of cultural relations with Russia is in all probability one of the most promising instruments to improve relations with that country. Although such a policy contains risks, the United States should be more prepared to take these risks than previously, for the advantages seem far to outweigh the dangers.

A footnote to this discussion must be added. If cultural relations with the Soviet Union have the potentialities that have been outlined, what of cultural relations with mainland China? No survey of American cultural policy abroad that pretends to air fundamental issues can neglect this question. In view of the present relations of the United States with Communist China, an extensive analysis of the significance and prospects of renewed cultural relations with that country would be out of place. Nevertheless, it is a mistake to treat all aspects of American relations with mainland China as though they depended on the question of diplomatic recognition of its government. At least some questions can be treated independently, and perhaps the most prominent of these is the question of cultural relations. For whatever one's views may be with regard to the recognition of the Chinese Communist Government, there are obviously grave perils in the indefinite continuance of a situation in which American citizens are cut off from direct communication with a very large proportion of the inhabitants of the same planet.

This has in fact been recognized by State Department officials, who, in their conversations with Chinese Communist representatives in Warsaw, have tried to arrange visits to China by American scholars and journalists. They have, however, regularly been rebuffed. At the present time, obviously, one can only be pessimistic that the leaders of Communist China will soon be receptive to the opening of their borders to Americans. However, a more public indication of willingness on the part of the United States Government to permit American citizens to visit China at their own risk is perhaps a desirable step toward the renewal of cultural contacts with that nation. The removal of passport restrictions would be a minimal action that would prejudge no other issue and would commit the United States Government to very little, but it would remove an impediment to communication that exists on the American side, and it would clear the air. Beyond this, the initiative for the practical conduct of cultural relations with China would have to come at the present time from private organizations and individuals.

RELATIONS WITH UNESCO AND OTHER INTERNATIONAL ORGANIZATIONS

The discussion so far has had to do mainly with bilateral arrangements between the United States and other countries. However, in many circumstances there is, of course, an option. Educational and cultural activities could in principle be conducted as parts of cooperative multinational programs, under the aegis of UNESCO or other international organizations. The case for working through such organizations is a strong one, but it is not an unqualified one.

Perhaps the most important contribution that an organization like UNESCO can make with regard to international educational and cultural programs is to remove from them the suspicion of "cultural imperialism." Whether just or unjust, this is a charge to which American educational and cultural programs are particularly subject. Where the immediate and most important purpose is to provide assistance in educational development, American money and talent may sometimes be more effectively deployed in a given country as part of an effort by an international agency in that country.

UNESCO is also useful as a center for communication in which nations with common educational and cultural problems can profit from one another's experience. In this capacity, as has been pointed out, it "has helped to formulate world standards for education, science, and cultural activities, which may assist member states to define their own pressing needs and to take remedial action." [3] UNESCO has also been useful in calling attention to some of the key educational and cultural issues involved in what Japanese scholars call "the North-South problem"—the relation between the industrialized and unindustrialized nations of the world, and the common problems that the nations in one category face in establishing communication and helpful relations with nations in the other. For all these reasons, support for UNESCO is obviously consonant with the objectives of American educational and cultural policy.

At the same time, however, UNESCO's relation to the sovereign states that compose the United Nations, and its dependence on their separate national concurrence with its policies, make it, in many respects, a multinational organization not an international one. In its daily activities, therefore, it faces political problems, and political problems of a particularly complicated sort. The formulation of a coherent educational policy for a given situation can sometimes be more difficult when there are many different national attitudes and interests involved than when an agreement must be reached between only two nations. The most deep-seated ideas and ideals of different cultures find expression in their approaches to education. Educational aid to a nation that asks for it

[3] Walter H. C. Laves and Charles A. Thomson, *UNESCO: Purpose, Progress, Prospects* (Indiana University Press, 1957), p. 345.

should not be delayed while a multinational team debates priorities at the level of cultural first principles. American support for experiments in multinational cooperation is justified, but the main thrust of the American effort, so far as educational development is concerned, should be directed toward helping the people in the affected country, and the question whether this goal will be pursued more effectively through bilateral or multilateral channels should be answered on a case-by-case basis.

In general, similar considerations appear to apply to the pursuit of other goals of educational and cultural cooperation, such as the bringing of educational systems together, the improvement of the context for communication, and the development of disciplined discourse among the intellectuals of different nations. The role of UNESCO and other international agencies with regard to the achievement of such purposes is obviously considerable. But the achievement of good bilateral arrangements also contributes to these purposes. There is good reason for a general policy of sympathetic support for UNESCO and other international agencies concerned with educational and cultural affairs. With regard to specific activities, however, they should be approached in a pragmatic spirit.

9

Principles and Practices

IN WRITING THIS STUDY, my main purpose, to repeat, has been to clarify principles. I have hoped to write a handbook that might be a useful guide to those who wish to think systematically about educational and cultural affairs, or who desire to act in this area with some reference to a criticized set of basic ideas.

Nevertheless, it is only reasonable to measure generalities against specifics. What are some of the practical proposals that might follow from the adoption of the general way of thinking that this study outlines? Some proposals have already been suggested in the course of the study. But it is appropriate in this last chapter to indicate, with regard to certain central questions, some of the practical implications of the general principles I have put forward.

BASIC REFORMS

If the analysis presented is in its main lines correct, there are three urgent needs that must be met if the conduct of American educational and cultural affairs abroad is to be placed on a sounder foundation. (1) Educational and cultural affairs need to be raised to a level of authority consonant with their significance for the relations of the American people with other nations. (2) The setting within which educational and cultural policy is formed and implemented needs to be changed. (3) A new, more cooperative, and more binding relationship needs to be formed between government and the private educational

132

and cultural communities. These provide, to my mind, the principal objectives toward which reforms should be directed. A summary word is in place about each of them.

The upgrading of educational and cultural relations. America's educational and cultural relations with other nations are immense in scope and are rapidly growing. They constitute a large part of our total commerce with other countries. In the long run, and in the not-so-long run, they may have as much significance for the well-being of the United States domestically, and for the course of international affairs, as do economic or political relations or the military balance of power. But the governmental arrangements that presently exist are not congruent with these facts and possibilities. Official American cultural activities on the international scene cannot now be described as the consequences of a coherent and comprehensive policy. They represent, on the whole, a collection of responses, sometimes brilliant, sometimes clumsy, to a set of immediate emergencies and opportunities. Decisions are made in scattered places, and usually by people at a relatively low level of authority. Most of the people who are charged with the conduct of educational and cultural relations in the field are subordinate officials in organizations whose central mission is other than educational and cultural.

A new environment for educational and cultural affairs. In addition to the fact that the importance of educational and cultural relations is not adequately reflected in existing governmental arrangements, another closely connected problem is posed by the fact that educational and cultural programs are conducted in environments that are not appropriate to their kind of activities. The problem is not a matter of personalities, but of basic administrative setting. Many officials of USIA, AID, and the Department of State have shown themselves cognizant of the special character and needs of educational and cultural programs. But in explaining and justifying these programs to the Congress or the public, they must inevitably do so in terms of the major purposes for which their agencies or departments exist. In recruiting people for these programs, they must fit them into organizations whose center of gravity lies elsewhere. In deciding by what criteria educational and cultural activities should be measured, it is almost impossible for them not to employ standards that belong to a quite different sort of activity. The result is that educational and cultural affairs are seen in a distorted perspective if they are seen at all.

A more effective relationship between government and the private educational and cultural communities. American educational and cultural programs abroad can be no better than the people who take part in them, and these people come, and must come, almost entirely from private life. On the one side, there has been inadequate recognition in governmental programs of the special requirements and attitudes of these people. On the other side, American universities, learned societies, and cultural organizations have made inadequate provision for meeting, in a planned way, American society's needs for the larger participation of such people in overseas activities. Better co-ordination between the government and nongovernment sectors cannot be achieved, however, by the classic technique of creating new committees addressed to this or that ad hoc problem. The basic conditions of cooperation have to be reformed. The educational, scholarly, and artistic worlds have to be drawn into international educational and cultural activities at the initial level at which policy and plans are formed. And they should be drawn into these activities under conditions in which they might develop, as organized entities, an active and continuing commitment.

In confronting these basic problems, a variety of practical measures come to mind. Some can be put into effect largely within the framework of existing administrative arrangements; some would require an alteration in the existing division of administrative responsibilities; some would require the creation of new agencies or organizations. In putting forward these ideas and suggestions, I would emphasize once again that I offer them largely for purposes of illustration. I believe they deserve consideration and debate, but it is possible that others will think of better ways to attain the objectives outlined.

IMPROVING THE POSITION OF
THE CULTURAL AFFAIRS OFFICER

On the assumption first, that essentially the same administrative arrangements that now exist will continue, CU, USIA, and AID will continue to be responsible for different sectors of educational and cultural affairs. And other federal agencies, such as the Office of Education and the National Science Foundation, will also have responsibilities in this area of foreign relations. Within this setting, changes could nevertheless be made in the position of the Cultural Affairs Officer in the field that would contribute significantly to the upgrading of educational and cultural affairs. Among the ideas that might be given consideration are the following.

The raising of the status of the Cultural Affairs Officer. The Cultural Affairs Officer should normally occupy a rank in the embassy hierarchy equal to that of the Public Affairs Officer. Career lines should be corrected so that cultural affairs offer as attractive a prospect to ambitious and able people as other fields of specialization in the foreign service.

The clarification of the task of the Cultural Affairs Officer. The Cultural Affairs Officer should be responsible for his own independent operation, and should have his own separate staff. Among other things, this would help to eliminate the ambiguity that currently characterizes the position of the Public Affairs Officer, who is expected, on one side, to explain day-to-day developments in United States foreign policy, and, on the other, to promote a sympathetic understanding of the less evanescent, nonpolitical aspects of American life. These two responsibilities are not usually compatible.

Libraries, book translation, and book publication should also be the principal responsibility of the Cultural Affairs Officer, though he should, of course, consult with his colleagues in the Public Affairs Section and in other divisions of the embassy in the discharge of these responsibilities. Such activities, where possible, should be housed separately from activities more directly concerned with the press and mass media.

With respect to leader and specialist grants, the Cultural Affairs Officer ought to have a special budget that he can use, subject to the authority of the Ambassador and CU, purely for the purpose of educational and cultural exchange strictly construed. Leader and specialist grants given for reasons not related to the central purposes of educational and cultural exchange are also necessary, but they should be administered separately.

Closely related to these suggestions is the need to determine more sharply than has so far been done whether the Cultural Affairs Officer's principal job is inside or outside his office. Paper work and the absence of adequate administrative and clerical assistance have meant that too many Cultural Affairs Officers are at present tied to their desks for too much of the time. Their most important tasks, however, can probably only be performed outside their offices.

Finally, and most important of all, it is desirable to clarify the criteria by which a Cultural Affairs Officer's work should be judged. The restatement of purposes attempted in Chapter 7 is one effort to indicate what such criteria should be. Fundamental to any realistic redefinition of the Cultural Affairs Officer's task must be the recognition that his work is long-range, and that it should not be subjected to the same timetable that applies to other embassy activities.

The extension of the responsibilities of the Cultural Affairs Officer. Due to the character of his work, an able Cultural Affairs Officer is centrally located with respect to a variety of educational and cultural problems, including many that fall outside his immediate area of responsibility. He has contacts with ministries, personal associations, and intimate knowledge of the local culture that people in other positions are not so likely to have. This should be reflected in the responsibilities assigned to him. He should, for example, be a regular member of committees concerned with AID educational programs, National Defense Education Act grants, or National Science Foundation projects, and whenever desirable, he should take a personal part in negotiations and other relations with foreign officials and nationals that are connected with such activities.

A flexible approach to the recruitment of Cultural Affairs Officers. Efforts, some of them successful, have already been made to recruit people of outstanding capacity for temporary duty as cultural representatives of the United States. Individuals of great prestige can sometimes be of considerable value in the position of Cultural Affairs Officer. Their major responsibility will not be to carry on the daily business of a cultural affairs office, but to act as spokesman for American scholarly and cultural life, and as intermediaries and interpreters between two cultures.

If this is the case, however, such people will usually require a strong back-up man to handle administrative matters; and it is desirable, in such circumstances, to give the top Cultural Affairs Officer a measure of discretion in choosing this assistant, since harmony and consistency within his office are essential to the success of his mission. It is perhaps desirable to add that individuals who serve in supporting positions should not be constrained to remain in such a role throughout their careers.

These recommendations also suggest the desirability of a more direct and strategic attack on the pivotal problem of the recruitment and training of Cultural Affairs Officers. A unification of the career services of the State Department and the USIA, which has long been under consideration, is now under way. This unification permits, perhaps, more concentrated attention to the development of a special Cultural Affairs career that will carry greater prestige and visibility, and ampler opportunities for high-level responsibility. In particular, there is a need for suitably ambitious programs of training for careers in cultural affairs, and for a fresh examination of the criteria by which people are chosen for such careers. The influx of people from academic life into cultural affairs after World War II must be assumed, for purposes of policy-making, to have been a piece of good luck that is not likely to repeat itself. If, in the future, people capable of representing American culture with knowledge and distinction are going to serve in cultural affairs positions—and there must be more such people than there have been— they are not likely to present themselves automatically. They will have to be sought out, they will have to find the job as a foreign service officer with a cultural affairs specialization an attractive prospect, and they will have to be carefully trained for it. Almost certainly, this will require the cooperation of universities, which alone provide the environment for a form of training whose fundament must be a liberal education.

As a more peripheral matter, further investigation might also be conducted into the possibility of creating special professorships within the exchange program. Men of outstanding scholarly reputations, combining capacities for lucid exposition with talents for diplomacy and personal relations, might be recruited for a period of a year or more. They might act as general cultural representatives in a given country, or might have the special task of helping to initiate programs of study in key universities. They would not, however, be Cultural Affairs Officers. Within the framework of their special assignments, they would have the freedom and independence enjoyed by exchange professors in general. The number of people competent to do this sort of job is probably limited. The results of past experiments have not been unfailingly encouraging. However, if the prestige and financial arrangements attached to such assignments were made commensurate with their importance, able people might be easier to find.

REALLOCATING EXISTING RESPONSIBILITIES

It is reasonable to hope that much might be accomplished even if only the recommendations described above were adopted. But consideration of the future of educational and cultural affairs should not be limited to such reforms as could be made without substantially altering the organizational framework that history, improvisation, and the bureaucratic struggles of the past have provided. For this would be to presuppose that the basic setting within which educational and cultural programs now take shape is essentially a satisfactory one. Is this so? The answer, on balance, must be "No."

Lodging central responsibility for educational and cultural affairs in the Department of State. Despite the talents and the organizational resources that it can bring to the tasks of presenting the facts about the United States, USIA's most important objectives are essentially out of keeping with those of educational and cultural affairs. Although USIA has long-range as well as short-range goals, the work of a USIA mission overseas is quite properly tied tightly to the programs of the embassy, and, of necessity, reflects tactical shifts in United States policy and changes in the international political weather. If these are also reflected in the work of the Cultural Affairs Officer—and due to his organizational connections, it is not easy for him to operate independently—his work loses the essential character it should have.

On the other hand, if the Cultural Affairs Officer's need for independence is recognized, as happens in some missions, and he is allowed to occupy a position insulated from the daily pressures of political and public relations, he is likely to find himself off in a corner of his own, without the organizational backing he needs. USIA does not provide the atmosphere or resources desirable for long-range educational thinking, and, even with the best of intentions, it provides a context for the discourse of scholars and intellectuals that tends to subordinate that discourse to immediate political considerations. Nor is it the best setting within which to establish close relations with the basic educational and scholarly institutions of other countries or to attract scholars and intellectuals into a full-scale commitment to international educational and cultural affairs.

To be sure, no matter what the auspices, any American educational or cultural program overseas is bound to be subject to the suspicion that it is politically or propagandistically motivated. This is true very often even when the program is privately financed. "Ford," "Rockefeller" and "Carnegie" are names that have definite political overtones in many places in the world. All such suspicions, however, are inevitably aggravated when an educational or cultural program is conducted by an agency whose main reason for being is political and propagandistic. USIA, in sum, does not appear to provide an appropriate setting for the conduct of educational and cultural relations.

The case for giving central authority over educational and cultural affairs to AID is no stronger. AID's interest in educational and cultural relations is specialized, and, at best, covers only one of the several purposes such relations should serve. The previous discussion indicates, indeed, that AID's special educational activities would themselves be improved if they were less project-oriented and enjoyed greater autonomy within the agency. The present head of the agency, David Bell, in a report to the President written when he was Director of the Bureau of the Budget, has spoken of the possibility of "a new kind of government research and development establishment which might be called a government institute." [1] John Gardner, in his special report on relations between AID and the universities, has recommended the establishment of a "National Institute for Educational and Technical Cooperation," which would be a separate corporate entity, though it would be ultimately responsible to the AID Administrator.[2] The thrust of the argument in this study is in the same general direction. AID's own educational programs should have greater independence from AID special technical projects, and should be more closely coordinated with the general educational and cultural effort. And that effort should not be too deeply embedded in the AID framework.

[1] *Report to the President on Government Contracting for Research and Development*, prepared by the Bureau of the Budget and referred to the Senate Committee on Government Operations, 87 Cong. 2 sess., S. Doc. 94 (Government Printing Office, May 17, 1962).

[2] John W. Gardner, *AID and the Universities*, A Report to the Administrator of the Agency for International Development (Education and World Affairs, 1964).

If we limit our attention to the bureaus and agencies that, in the past, have been principally concerned with educational and cultural policy abroad, these considerations appear to suggest that primary responsibility for educational and cultural affairs should be lodged in the Department of State. To be sure, the department is already extremely large, and the upgrading and extension of educational and cultural programs would make it still larger. Its career service does not consist of men whose central interest lies in education, scholarship, or the arts. The department is an organization, furthermore, whose main focus of attention is inevitably on crises and the prevention of crises. From time to time, too, it must sanction or threaten the use of force. And it is always involved in tactical maneuvers, and in taking sides, implicitly or explicitly, in political controversies elsewhere. This is obviously not the most congenial setting for educational and cultural activities.

These handicaps, however, can be partly overcome by further reinforcing the independence, within the department, of the Bureau of Educational and Cultural Affairs. By giving the Board of Foreign Scholarships an independent staff, the autonomy and integrity of educational and cultural exchange could be still further protected and enhanced. On the whole, the argument for lodging principal responsibility for educational and cultural affairs in the Department of State is more persuasive than for lodging it in any of the other agencies that have shared this responsibility. The department offers desirable prestige and protection, and its structure makes it more capable of treating educational and cultural affairs as a separate and largely autonomous activity.

The creation of an Under-Secretary of State for Educational and Cultural Affairs. The argument would be even more persuasive, however, if the position of Assistant Secretary for Educational and Cultural Affairs were raised to the Under-Secretary level. The position of the Cultural Affairs Officer in the field is inevitably influenced by the prestige and authority of the office in Washington most responsible for what he does. At present, there is no official in Washington at a high level of authority who has major responsibility for American educational and cultural affairs abroad. The Assistant Secretary of State for Educational and Cultural Affairs does not have the same status, and normally does not have the same access to the President, for example, that the Director of the United States Information Agency has. Indeed, within the Department of State, his position is likely to carry less authority than that of other Assistant Secretaries, who are responsible for dealing with the crises that constitute the most pressing business of the department.

This is a disconcerting anomaly in view of the importance of educational and cultural affairs to the long-range interests of the United States. It converts into something close to a dead letter the present Executive directive to the Secretary of State to provide leadership and policy guidance in regard to educational and cultural affairs. Moreover, educational and cultural affairs, like economic and political affairs, are a *continuing aspect* of foreign relations, and if we conduct our reckonings by the proper time span, they approach economic and political affairs in importance. The desirability of recognizing their co-ordinate position by creating the post of Under-Secretary for Educational and Cultural Affairs should be considered.

With the creation of this position, needless to say, there should go proportionate authority to create guiding policy for the over-all field of educational and cultural affairs. The official occupying this position should also be given reasonable discretion in selecting the people who work for him, and Cultural Affairs Officers in the field should come directly under his supervision and control, rather than being drawn, as at present, from another agency.

It must be emphasized, however, that the above recommendation rests on the presupposition that the basic structure of Executive agencies will remain largely as it is. It is conceivable, for example, that at some future date the Office of Education might be raised to the level of a department, and given cabinet status. Obviously, in the absence of information about the character and powers of this hypothetical department, it is not possible to say whether it would provide a better home for educational and cultural affairs than the Department of State. But if this or a similar happening should occur, the case for locating principal responsibility for the operation of educational and cultural programs within the Department of State would be properly subject to reconsideration.

REORGANIZING EDUCATIONAL AND CULTURAL EXCHANGE

The suggestions made up to this point rest on the assumption that proposals for reform of the federal government's effort in international educational and cultural affairs will be limited to those that can be adopted without creating new organizational entities. In the final analysis, however, consideration should be given to the thesis that only the creation of such a new entity is likely fully to meet the urgent needs presently making reform desirable.

The creation of a semiautonomous foundation for educational and cultural exchange. Although the Department of State provides one suitable environment for the conduct of educational and cultural affairs, and although reforms such as those recommended in this chapter could make it an even better environment, the Department also has certain handicaps as a setting for educational and cultural activities. Educational and cultural programs have only a peripheral relationship to the department's most pressing concerns and tend to be submerged under the weight of its main activities.

It is against this background that consideration might be given to the establishment of a semiautonomous foundation that would have central responsibility for planning and implementing the United States Government's educational and cultural effort abroad. Such a foundation, which could perhaps receive financial support from both public and private sources, as the Smithsonian Institution has, would provide the government with an agency for cultural exchange possessing some of the flexibility and other attributes of a private nonprofit corporation. Its governing board should be composed of government officials representative of concerned departments and agencies, such as the Department of State and the Office of Education, and of individuals representative of education, scholarship, the arts, and the sciences. The latter should be "representative" in the strict technical sense of the term. They should be chosen, that is to say, by key scholarly and educational organizations in American society that are themselves representative organizations. An illustrative list would include the American Council of Learned Societies, the Social Science Research Council, the National Academy of Sciences, the American Council on Education, the Association of State Universities and Land Grant Colleges, and the American Association of University Professors. Comparable organizations, representative of people in the arts, literature, music, dance, and theatre, should also be included.

This would mean that the educational and cultural communities were consulted as equal partners at the highest levels in the formation of international educational and cultural policy. Such policy would then have an authority, and a possible resonance, that it does not possess under present conditions. Indeed, the very process of making policy would involve the educational and cultural communities in a large commitment to carry out such policy. Of course, the difficulties of establishing cooperative arrangements among universities, learned societies, or artistic groups are notorious. Perhaps for this very reason, the hypothesis is worth exploring that such cooperation might be easier to achieve if a proper organizational context were provided by high governmental authority.

A semiautonomous foundation would presumably be staffed by a core group of career officials, drawn in part from the university, publishing, museum, and foundation worlds. A reasonable proportion of its representatives in the field as well as in Washington would belong to this permanent staff. The foundation would also have a reserve staff, for duty abroad and at home, composed of people who alternated between periods of a year or two as its employees or representatives and longer periods of work in private educational or cultural institutions. It is to be hoped that universities and professional organizations would regard such service as normal and commendable parts of a professional career, and would appropriately reward those who undertook such service. It is also to be hoped that proper financial and other assistance would be given to universities and professional organizations to make it possible for them to take this posture.

Although the principle would continue to be recognized in each country that the United States Ambassador's authority extended over representatives of all United States Government agencies, the representatives of this foundation would operate with considerable autonomy, as is now the case, for example, with Peace Corps representatives. Whether they would be officially accredited as attachés of the embassy would depend on the rules of the host nation and on purely pragmatic considerations that vary from country to country. Moreover, the creation of new positions in the field should not be taken to imply that the presently existing post of Cultural Affairs Officer should everywhere be abolished. Nomenclature might be changed, but the creation of this new position would free the man presently occupying the position of Cultural Affairs Officer so that he could serve more largely as cultural reporter, analyst, and liaison man for the Ambassador and Washington. Under present arrangements, the important task of reportage is skimped or neglected. Once again, pragmatic considerations that presumably differ from country to country should determine whether the old position of Cultural Affairs Officer should be retained.

Inevitably, a foundation such as here discussed invites comparisons with the British Council. There are analogies; but precedents drawn from the American scene are in fact more pertinent and are increasingly numerous. The Smithsonian Institution, for example, which antedates the British Council, is a prototype of the kind of organization here envisaged. In many respects, the National Science Foundation and the National Academy of Sciences also offer useful precedents. In the relative independence it enjoys in the field, and in its careful separation of its tasks from more immediate political and propagandistic goals, the Peace Corps as well presents an apposite analogy. And in the independence and general supervisory powers assigned to the Board of Foreign Scholarships the seed of what is here being discussed is present.

An immediately relevant analogy is offered by the bill to establish a National Foundation on the Arts and Humanities, sent by President Johnson to the Congress on March 10, 1965. [3] This bill calls for the establishment of a foundation supported by both private and public funds. It is to be governed by a board composed of public officials and private citizens, including representatives of such organizations as the National Science Foundation, the Library of Congress, and the Department of State. It would be a mistake at this early stage in the development of an idea to suggest that the scheme for the Educational and Cultural Exchange Foundation here envisaged should be a duplicate in every respect of the scheme for the Foundation on the Arts and Humanities. Nor is it necessary to conceive it as a separate entity, although that is possible. But it might also be attached to the Humanities Foundation, to the National Science Foundation, to the two together, or to

[3] Since the completion of this manuscript (June 1965), the National Foundation on the Arts and Humanities was established by law (P.L. 209, 89 Cong. 1 sess.) Sept. 29, 1965.

some other existing agency, such as the National Academy of Sciences, properly modified and extended. The details are at this point not so important as the principle. That principle is implicit in practices to which the federal government, confronted by the problems raised by the partnership of government with private research and scholarship, has already begun to turn. The principle remains to be extended to the important field of international educational and cultural affairs.

The establishment of such a foundation, it may be hoped, would remove educational and cultural activities from a short-term perspective, and relieve those responsible for them from the burden of justifying them from year to year. Congressional examination of the work of such a foundation would of course still be necessary, but there would be greater reason to expect that this examination would be conducted in terms, and in a time perspective, appropriate to educational and cultural activities. Coordination with the policies of the State Department, AID, and other government agencies would still be possible, but it could be conducted under conditions assuring that educational and cultural activities will not be force-fitted to purposes unsuitable to them.

More positively, such an organization, capable of taking an overview of educational and cultural policy as a whole, would complement American planning in diplomatic, economic, and military spheres. And by making it possible for relations to be established between a high-level, self-sustaining American educational organization and binational commissions elsewhere, this foundation would strengthen the work of these commissions and simplify and rationalize the process of international educational planning and exchange. Last, the people who, in the end, must do the work so far as educational and cultural programs are concerned would be represented in the determination of basic policy. An organization would exist that they would regard as their own.

The place of the federal government in international educational and cultural relations. The question can be raised, of course, whether it would not be better to go the whole way and to remove the federal government from the scene, leaving educational and cultural affairs entirely in private hands. The degree to which the government should participate and the kind of participation it should undertake, is, indeed, a matter that would be subject to considerable reconsideration if a foundation of the kind here proposed were to be established. Such a foundation, it is possible, could be more effective by providing private institutions with important forms of direction and assistance, rather than by conducting educational or cultural exchange programs of its own. In any event, much that is now taken for granted would surely be subject to review. However, no matter what new arrangements may be made for the organization of the federal government's educational and cultural affairs, a fundamental fact is bound to remain. The federal government will still be directly responsible for only a portion of American international educational and cultural affairs. Accordingly, the proposal to establish a new semiautonomous agency enjoying a larger measure of central authority is to be understood only within the framework of a larger pluralism. There is no question of a monopoly of power, or of a monolithic central authority.

In these terms, the question is simply whether the federal government has any place among the myriad organizations concerned with American educational and cultural relations with foreign countries. To me there seems only one possible answer. The federal government should occupy an important place. It is peculiarly capable of providing the leadership, and of stimulating the movement toward coordination and planning, which American educational and cultural affairs so badly need. And there would be something inappropriate, symbolically as well as practically, in the withdrawal of the federal government from an active role in educational and cultural affairs.

The symbolic issue is as important as any. Federal support and encouragement of educational and cultural institutions and of their international ramifications is the expression of a national commitment. To the extent that the United States Government gives this support and encouragement under conditions that preserve the autonomy and dignity of these institutions, it announces that our society regards them not only as instruments of policy but as the independent expressions of a free civilization, to be prized as ends in themselves. American educational and cultural institutions represent a side of our civilization by which, as much as by anything else, its quality is measured. A substantial and coherent federal effort in international educational and cultural affairs—an effort which has been foreshadowed, but only foreshadowed, by what has so far been done—would do as much as anything could to set our best values before the world, and to present them in the perspective in which they ought properly to be viewed.

THE PRIMACY OF PRINCIPLES

Practical reforms can generate an illusion of change while in fact they change little or nothing. As I remarked at the outset of this study, it has not been my central purpose to make proposals about the mechanics and organization of the federal government's international educational and cultural activities. My central purpose has been to bring fundamental issues into focus, and to discuss the matters of principle that might help us to think these issues through.

To be sure, principles that carried no practical implications or that challenged no established patterns of action would be little more than sententious platitudes. But the argument in this book should not be thought to stand or fall on the practical suggestions that have been made in this final chapter. There may be other suggestions, and better ones, that would also be consistent with the argument that has been set forth. It is even possible (though more difficult) to think that the scattered and largely ad hoc arrangements that now exist are triumphs of ingenuity, and that, in a complex and many-sided society like the United States, with its special traditions, they organize all the interests, needs, skills, and perspectives that are represented in educational and cultural affairs better than any new scheme of organization is likely to do. But it is not possible to think that either existing practical arrangements or new ones are likely to be effective unless they are informed by an examined body of thought, and unless this body of thought has some claim to validity.

United States educational and cultural commerce with other nations comprises a significant portion of its total commerce with them. It is significant for its sheer magnitude, and it is even more significant for its controlling influence over the course of the affairs of the United States and mankind. It is a neglected dimension of foreign affairs, and one that has occupied an unduly subordinate position in the total spectrum of American efforts abroad. Educational and cultural affairs, to be properly conducted, must have their own setting and must be measured by their own proper standards. They are misunderstood, mismanaged, and mismarried when this is not the case.

A firmer and more sympathetic grasp of these principles, not only by a few government officials, but by the American public at large, is necessary if American educational and cultural activities abroad are to realize more fully the potentialities implicit in them. This, more than anything else, is the practical reform to which this study points.

STRUCTURE OF A USIS POST * **

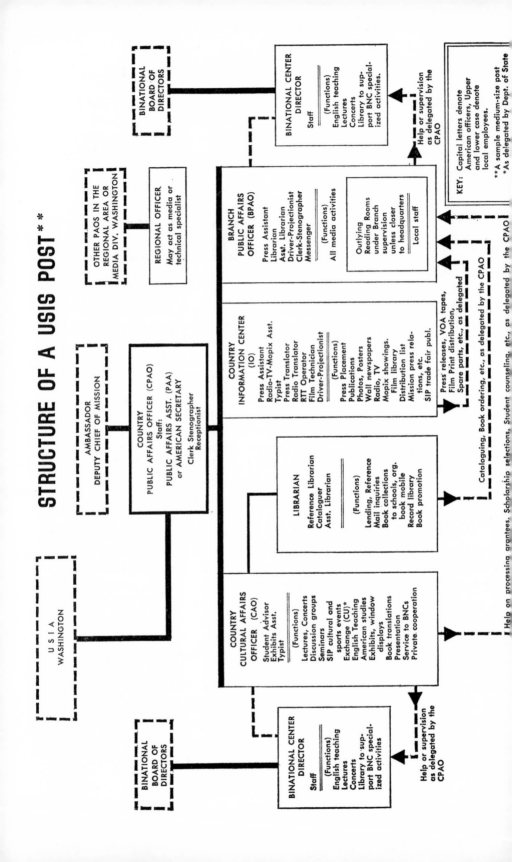

USIA
WASHINGTON

OTHER PAOS IN THE
REGIONAL AREA OR
MEDIA DIV. WASHINGTON

REGIONAL OFFICER
May act as media or
technical specialist

AMBASSADOR
DEPUTY CHIEF OF MISSION

COUNTRY
PUBLIC AFFAIRS OFFICER (CPAO)
Staff:
PUBLIC AFFAIRS ASST. (PAA)
or AMERICAN SECRETARY
Clerk Stenographer
Receptionist

BINATIONAL
BOARD OF
DIRECTORS

BINATIONAL CENTER
DIRECTOR

Staff
_____
(Functions)
English teaching
Lectures
Concerts
Library to sup-
port BNC special-
ized activities

Help or supervision
as delegated by the
CPAO

COUNTRY
CULTURAL AFFAIRS
OFFICER (CAO)

Student Advisor
Exhibits Asst.
Typist
_____
(Functions)
Lectures, Concerts
Discussion groups
Seminars
SIP cultural and
  sports events
Exchange (CU)*
English Teaching
American studies
Exhibits, window
  displays
Book translations
Presentation
Service to BNCs
Private cooperation

LIBRARIAN

Reference Librarian
Cataloguer
Asst. Librarian
_____
(Functions)
Lending, Reference
Mail inquiries
Book collections
  to schools, org.
  book mobile
Record library
Book promotion

COUNTRY
INFORMATION CENTER
(IO)

Press Assistant
Radio-TV-Mopix Asst.
Typist
Press Translator
Radio Translator
RTT Operator
Film Technician
Driver-Projectionist
_____
(Functions)
Press Placement
Publications
Photos, Posters
Wall newspapers
Radio, TV
Mopix showings,
  Film library
Distribution list
Mission press rela-
  tions, etc.
SIP trade fair publ.

BRANCH
PUBLIC AFFAIRS
OFFICER (BPAO)

Press Assistant
Librarian
Asst. Librarian
Driver-Projectionist
Clerk-Stenographer
Messenger
_____
(Functions)
All media activities

Outlying
Reading Rooms
under Branch
supervision
unless closer
to headquarters
_____
Local staff

BINATIONAL
BOARD OF
DIRECTORS

BINATIONAL CENTER
DIRECTOR

Staff
_____
(Functions)
English teaching
Lectures
Concerts
Library to sup-
port BNC special-
ized activities.

Help or supervision
as delegated by the
CPAO

Press releases, VOA tapes,
Film Print distribution,
Spare parts, etc., as delegated

Cataloguing, Book ordering, etc., as delegated by the CPAO

Help on processing grantees, Scholarship selections, Student counseling, etc., as delegated by the CPAO

KEY: Capital letters denote
American officers, Upper
and lower case denote
local employees.

*A sample medium-size post
**As delegated by Dept. of State

Index

149